# WELCOME

You may write down your learnings, Goals, Affirmations, etc. bellow after finishing this Book.

*This Book belongs to -*

_____

# PREFACE

INDIA, the most populous Country in this World having Youth Population as the highest among any other age group. But despite of it, the harsh Reality is very different from what it can be expected.

Our maximum population is still struggling for the basic needs which are required to live a simple and healthy life. Many among them are BPLs (Bellow Poverty Line) i.e., they are not even assured to have two meals a day! As a matter of fact, "Poor people are becoming Poorer and Rich people are becoming Richer".

The reason behind this is very simple, which is LACK OF KNOWLEDGE, CONFIDENCE and DISCIPLINE. Whereas, Rich people always have a tendency to look after these parameters as and whenever possible, this ultimately helps them to achieve their Goals.

# About the Author

*Author of this book is a boy of India who started writing Books after his completion of School studies in urge to keep his feelings, facts, conclusions in front of the Society.*

# ACKNOWLEDGEMENT

I would like to acknowledge my sincere gratitude towards my Parents, my Teachers and every source of knowledge which made me capable of writing this Book.

I would like to thank my lovely readers and followers who always helped me to enhance my writing skills and motivated me to always give my best for every Book to be finished.

This Book will surely help the people among every stage of life to create financial literacy and discipline within themselves and will be able to live wealthy and happy life.

It is strongly recommended for the millennial and retirees to get maximum benefits from this Book.

I welcome and wish you all a Wealthy and Happy future ahead!

# CONTENTS

1. Understanding the Basics....6-16

2. START-UP Savings……….17-40

3. Goal Planning…………......41-74

4. Risk Profile Assessment....75-88

5. Insure Your Future………...89-96

6. Mutual Funds…….……...97-157

7. Introducing Stock Market……………..……...158-183

# Understanding the Basics

*"Money is not everything, but Money can provide you many things!"*

The above said lines are mostly relatable to everyone's life. Yes, Money is important. But have we ever given importance to learn and acquire the knowledge/skills for accumulation of wealth and becoming Rich. No, we always just tried to get money and have it by any possible means irrespective of it being legal/illegal. The reason behind it is also very clear, as Money gives you Power and they work proportional to each other. Due to which many fraudsters trap such people who are just mad on money and they are very easily convinced in false beliefs which leads to an ultimate loss of the remaining amount which they had themselves.

Well, fortunately we have Cyber Cell department of Police which looks after such Crimes and their main objective is to recover your loss as soon as possible but if you get late on complaining, there is less chance of money recovery.

Personal Finance is something which needs to be taught at an early age, better to be at an intermediate school level. Even parents can also contribute their knowledge and help their child to understand the basics of money matter from the very scratch of it.

Money is a medium of exchange of goods and services at their own cost which defines its value. But, money doesn't have its own value as a medium of exchange. So, the separate currencies were introduced in every part of this world and the Currency of India is 'Indian Rupees'.

From the very first when Indian Rupees were introduced, it had gone through many changes in terms of physical structure and the amount of Money. Coins are the oldest among them which had also gone through many alterations and modifications after which today we have coins of ₹1, ₹2, ₹5, ₹10, ₹20. These are the most commonly used coins in today's Indian Market, some of them (*Paisa*) are no more used and some are yet to be introduced. Along with coins there are Indian Rupee Notes which are also used in the markets as of ₹10, ₹20, ₹50, ₹100, ₹200, ₹500, ₹2000 are commonly used and more variations may be observed in the Future.

The value, structure and other aspects are regulated by the Money Regulatory Board of India which is represented by the RBI (Reserve Bank of India).

If closely observed on the Indian Rupee Note then it can be clearly seen that there's a statement written on it which says that "I PROMISE TO PAY THE BEARER THE SUM OF *Amount* RUPEES" with a signature of RBI Governor bellow the lines. It simply means that whoever holds this particular amount of money can buy the goods/services and it's then the liability of RBI to pay the bearer of goods/services at its cost. Further there are many unique things in every single note which depicts its individuality.

Apart from the fact that these are used as a medium of exchange, they are usually kept in a Bank which is a place where different money related activities are performed and is the very first step towards Personal Finance. A long time back, Banks were just a place to save and lend money.

But, today things have changed a lot as now, Banks not only offer to save and lend money but they also provide numerous facilities to their customers as on the large scale of SAVINGS, LENDING, INSURING and INVESTING. Each of them also includes many sub-categories which differentiate one Bank from another on the ground of their customer service and performance.

There are mainly 4 types of Banks:-

I. <u>CENTRAL BANK</u> – The controller, regulator and head of all the Banks in a Country is known as Central Bank. It controls the management and major system of banking services. It regulates the Monetary Policies on a National level. They are fully governed by the government of that Nation. Ex.- RBI in India

II. <u>COMERCIAL BANK</u> – These are mostly the Banks which performs Retail Banking for their customers and provides all types of banking services which helps people to manage their Personal and Corporate Finances.

These are of two types –

a) <u>Public Sector Banks</u> –

These are the Banks which are governed by the Government of that Nation due to holding of more than 50% of share of that particular Bank.

b) <u>Private Sector Bank</u> –

These are the Banks which are governed by the people who established and founded it along with holding maximum share of particular Bank.

COOPERATIVE BANK – These are small to medium scale a self-service type organization which provides and facilitates limited financial services and they only provide those to their own members or the owner/s of the Bank. They are mainly known for their lending of Money at very low interest rates.

III. SPECIALIZED BANK – These are the Banks which are specially opened for benefit in specific fields in finance management and provides banking services in India, there are 3 major sector specific specialized Banks as follows –

   a) SIDBI – Small Industries Development Bank of India, it provides financial assistance to small and medium scale Business.

b) **EXIM Bank** – Export and Import Bank, it provides Loans or Financial assistance for exporting and importing of goods across overseas in foreign countries.

c) **NABARD** – National Bank for Agriculture and Rural Development as the name suggests, it is more specific in development across the rural areas, villagers and farmers in the field of Agriculture for their financial assistance.

As now we have come across different types of Banks, we will be focusing more on the 'Commercial Banks' as because these banks are mostly used by the people to manage their Finances. As discussed earlier that these are of two types – Public Sector and Private Sector Banks. A person has always a choice to select the Bank as per the suitability which fulfills all the requirements.

After selecting the Bank, you can open your Account as 'SAVINGS' Account or 'CURRENT' Account. Basically, these two accounts are the Primary Bank Accounts from which you can start your journey of Personal Finance and avail major financial services directly/indirectly linked with it.

But as the name suggests, these two Accounts are a bit different from each other. As if you open a 'CURRENT' Account, then it is meant for your frequent and current expenses and thus has no limit on your transactions but it do not have interest rates given and thus, no tax is applied in this Account. Moreover, if you are eligible then you may opt for an OD (Overdraft Account) it provides an extra surplus amount as a loan at prescribed interest rates. Mainly, 'CURRENT' Accounts are preferred by high pay salaried employs and businessmen due to tax and transaction benefits.

Now, if you open a 'SAVINGS' Account then there are certain restrictions on transactions whereas few limitations on deposits and withdrawals but it provides a fix interest rate on the principal amount kept in the account and the tax are charged on the interest gain according to the income tax slab.

'Always remember, before opening an Account in any Bank first try to analyze the position of that Bank in terms of monetary regulations. For example, suppose a new Bank has came into market and is offering an interest rate which is far more than offered by other Banks in average. Then it might be an alarming situation. In these circumstances, if you are capable of doing a proper analysis then it's good or else it is better to switch into more renowned and trusted Banks which provides a higher security and safety to your Money.

NOTE – If you already have an account in a Bank which has gone Bankrupt then also there's a provision of recovery to some extent as per the Union Budget 2021, our Finance Minister has declared that in case a Bank fails or withdrawals from the Bank are stopped due to financial pressure on the Bank, the depositors will be able to get immediate access to their deposit insurance amount up to 5 Lakhs under the 'DEPOSIT INSURANCE AND CREDIT GUARENTEE CORPORATION ACT, 1961 DICGC ACT'.

# START-UP Savings

*"Money saved is Money earned!"*

We have now crossed our first step of opening a Bank Account and will move towards savings and investing them gradually. As said earlier, two types of Account can be created by an individual as CURRENT/SAVINGS Account.

Now the choice can vary from person to person but both of them have their own requirements. If considering opening a SAVINGS Account for the reason being commonly used and with a benefit of 2-3% interest rates is certainly ok but not beneficial. As there are several factors to it and the most common factor to it is the Tax deducted on interest earned on the sum which ranges anywhere between 5% - 30% as per the Income Tax Slab.

Hence, whatever your income may be, if it falls under the slab rate will be charged Tax accordingly.

Similarly, there's a very important factor which usually gets neglected or underestimated during any financial planning which leads to an unrealistic approach and outcomes that can be drastic in future. But, before jumping into this topic we have to first understand the basics of 'interest rates' and the rule of 'compounding'.

So now let's understand that why do we get 'interest' on our principal amount deposited in a Bank/Financial Institute and how we are benefited from it. Interest rates are managed by RBI through its Monetary Policies; these rates can vary from different Banks and is the primary element of lending money.

As if a Bank provides Loan to the Public or Institutions then the principal amount needs to be given back in small fractions along with the interest rates applicable to it within the given time period. In this process we lend money from the Bank and thus need to pay interest on that amount.

Now, interest on deposits is just opposite of this process. As here, Bank needs money which it can also get from RBI at a very nominal rate of interest but Bank also needs to look after its customers because unless a person/institute open up an Account in the Bank, till then the Bank cannot provide the loan to their customers and will not be able to earn extra money from the interest rates charged on the loan amount which is required for the business. Thus, banks provide interest on Deposits as to attract their customers to become their Bank Account holders so that in future if they require extra money as Loan then the Bank can easily avail the loan to them and earn interest from the money given to the account holder as a loan.

Mainly Depository Accounts which are directly provided by the Banks are the FDs (Fixed Deposits) and RDs (Recurring Deposits), the method of savings is also the same as the name suggests.

In FDs we save a chunk of money for a certain time period in which the applicable interest on that amount is accumulated at particular intervals and is given along with the principal amount or Total amount deposited at the time of maturity.

To understand it more clearly, we will take examples –

In case of an FD, assume you have ₹10,000 and you want it to make it a fixed deposit for 2yrs at an interest rate of 5% which is compounded quarterly (in most of the banks)

Then, it will be – $[A = P \times (1 + r/n)^{(n \times t)}]$

Where,

(A) = FD Maturity Amount

(P) = Principal Amount

(t) = Total time in years

(n) = No. of compounding periods per year

(r) = Nominal Annual interest rate

So here according to the assumptions it will be –

(P) = ₹10,000

(t) = 2 years

(n) = 4 (a quarter consists of 3 months)

(r) = 5%

Thus, $[A = P \times (1 + r/n)^{(n \times t)}]$

Or, $A = ₹10{,}000 \times (1 + 5\%/4)^{(4 \times 2)}$ = **₹11,045**

So, total interest accumulated will be – ₹11,045 - ₹10,000 = *₹1,045*

In case of RD, assume you save ₹2,000 every month and you want to continue it for 2 years at an interest rate of 5% compounded quarterly.

Then, it will be –

$M = R\,[(1+i)^n - 1] \div [1 - (1+i)^{-1/3}]$

Where, (M) = RD maturity value

(R) = Monthly installment

(n) = Number of quarters

(i) = Interest rate/400

So here, according to the assumptions it will be –

(R) = ₹2,000

(n) = 8 (4 quarters in a year)

(i) = 5÷400

Thus, M=R $[(1+i)^n - 1] \div [1-(1+i)^{-1/3}]$

M = $2000[(1+5÷400)^8 - 1] \div [1-(1+5÷400)^{-1/3}]$
= ₹50,570

Total investment = ₹2,000× 24 (months) = ₹48,000 and Interest earned = ₹50,570 - ₹48000 = ₹2570

Both of the savings method discussed above are based on the compound interest which was calculated in the previous examples of RDs and FDs. Interest calculated on any savings/investment are of two types mainly the 'Simple Interest' and the 'Compound Interest' in which the compound interest is more profitable and beneficial in comparison to the simple interest because of the reason that is the working principles of both phenomenon.

In simple words, if you have done your Savings by the method of Simple Interest then according to the calculation you will get a fixed amount of interest regardless of the time you saved money i.e., say you save ₹10,000 in a FD for 2 years at 5% of simple interest.

Then, the maturity amount will be,

$A = P(1 + r \times t)$

Where, (A) = Total amount accumulated

(P) = Principal Amount

(r) = Rate of Return    (t) = Time invested

So, it will be - $P(1 + r \times t)$

Or, $A = ₹10,000 \times (1 + 5\% \times 2) = ₹11,000$

Interest Earned will be –

₹11,000 - ₹10,000 = *₹1,000* which means ₹500 per year of interest gain.

Whereas, in case of Compound Interest you can try it yourself with the same data and you will then find the difference.

Well, the results calculated will have a difference in which the amount accumulated by the Compound Interest will be greater than the Simple Interest. The reason is because Compound Interest works on a principle that on the first year of investment, the interest earned will become the principal amount in the next year and accordingly you get the benefit of Compounding on interest earned and here the Time is the greatest factor amongst all and that's the reason it is said that *"The earlier you start, the greater you get."* Even the Albert Einstein once said that *"Compounding is the world's $8^{th}$ wonder, who knows it earns it and those who don't they pay for it."*

There are several options provided by the Bank and they are very profitable as well as beneficial to create a wealthy future with a proper management, but as it is less in savings and more towards investing perspective, we will discuss about those in our upcoming chapters.

Now beside these savings in a traditional Bank we can also prefer to open up an Account in Post Office as POSA or IPPB known as (Post Office Savings Account) or (India Post Payments Bank Account). These two are quite similar and have their own benefits as if said in a nutshell then POSA is the oldest Account type which started after the independence of India. It can't be opened online and needs to be open in a Post Office but it does not have any upper ceiling of money to be kept in the account and comes with an annual interest rate of 4% on Savings Account and all other savings/investment methods are also available to it. But the money kept in that account cannot be transferred to any other Bank, it can only be transferred to any other Post Office Savings Account.

Whereas, the IPPB can be opened online with zero balance and it becomes fully activated once the KYC (Know Your Customer) is done. But it has an upper limit of ₹1,00,000 which can be kept in that account and annual interest rate on Savings Account is 2.0% (as of 1$^{st}$ June 2022) but it provides the feature of transferring money from and to any Bank across the Country and it also provides access to all the Savings/Investment options as provided in POSA.

So, now you must be thinking that both the Accounts, either it is POSA or IPPB comes with some benefits and limits. But, if I say that you can get both the advantages from these two Accounts, Yes it is possible.

As if a person opens up a Digital Savings Account in IPPB which can be done online and then the KYC needs to be done within 1 year and at the time of doing KYC of IPPB Account you may open up an POSA Savings Account in the Post Office and then complete the KYC of IPPB Account to fully activate all the features and then link your POSA and IPPB Account after which you will get full access to all the features of both the Accounts.

We are now totally prepared to proceed with better alternatives of Savings option provided by the Post Office. Apart from FDs and RDs, Post Office provides us various alternatives for several goals associated with one's life in which most of them are more of a purpose driven investment rather than a normal savings for preserving and growing the corpus.

We shall discuss each and every investment options provided by the Post Office in our upcoming chapters but for now focusing on the savings perspective, we will be analyzing the benefits of the two most popular savings option provided by the Post Office which are NSC and KVP.

NSC (National Savings Certificate) is one of the most popular savings plan offered by the Post Office for creating the habit of Savings in every individual and to help them in achieving their financial goals in a more systematic manner.

It is often said to start early to be able to grow larger corpus in the upcoming future. So how early it should be, the answer to this question is as early as you can as technically it is said whenever you start earning which usually happen in between 20-30 or in average of 25 years of age. But, the eligibility criteria starts from the age of 18 years and usually at this age everyone gets a pocket money which can be invested to generate wealth and due to the power of compounding it creates a major effect in the growth of the invested corpus.

Let's now discuss some salient features of this Savings scheme –

    a) It has tenure of 5 years.
    b) The rate of interest (ROI) is 7.7% per annum (as of April-June 2023) compounded annually.

c) It can be transferred once in a lifetime.

d) Loan can be availed against the scheme against its Certificate.

e) It can also be opened in the name of a minor but can only be accessed by an adult supervising the account.

f) Minimum investment required is ₹1,000 and there is no maximum limit.

We have now understood the basics of NSC and a detailed study will be done further, to mathematically observe the growth in the Principal amount invested.

We will now observe two scenarios based on the Age difference in this instrument of savings.

## **SCENARIO – (A)**

A 50 year old man wants to save some money for his savings at the age of 60 through NSC and invests ₹120000 for 5 years and again for next 5 years to achieve the retirement age.

In this case, as we know R.O.I of N.S.C is 7.7%p.a compounded annually.

Principal Amount - ₹120000
Tenure – 5 years (up to age 60) here the person is 50yro so, it will be 2 times.

Compound Interest (CI) will be –
Principal Amount (P) × (1+ROI %)$^{Time}$

Or, C.I. - ₹120000× (1+7.7%)$^5$ = ₹173884

In next 5 years, it will be –
C.I. - ₹173884× (1+7.7%)$^5$ = ₹251964

Thus at the age of 60, the total corpus will be **₹251964.**

## SCENARIO – (B)

A 20 year old boy who is also saving for his retirement through the NSC and invests ₹12000 saved from his pocket Money repeatedly for 5 years until he attends the 60 years of age.

In this case, as we know N.S.C. (R.O.I) is 7.7%p.a compounded annually.

Principal Amount – 12000

Tenure – 5 years (up to 60) here, the person is 20yro so, it will be 8 times.

C.I. = ₹12000× $(1+7.7\%)^5$ = ₹17388... ($1^{st}$)

In the next 5 years, it will be –

C.I. - ₹17388× $(1+7.7\%)^5$ = ₹25196... ($2^{nd}$)

In the next 5 years, it will be –

C.I. - ₹25196× $(1+7.7\%)^5$ = ₹36510..... ($3^{rd}$)

In the next 5 years, it will be –

C.I. - ₹36510× $(1+7.7\%)^5$ = ₹52904.... ($4^{th}$)

In the next 5 years, it will be –

C.I. - ₹52904 × (1+7.7%)$^5$ = ₹76660…. (5$^{th}$)

In the next 5 years, it will be –

C.I. - ₹76660 × (1+7.7%)$^5$ = ₹111083… (6$^{th}$)

In the next 5 years, it will be –

C.I. - ₹111083 × (1+7.7%)$^5$ = ₹160963. (7$^{th}$)

In the next 5 years, it will be –

C.I. - ₹160963 × (1+7.7%)$^5$ = ₹233241. (8$^{th}$)

Thus, the maturity value at the age of 60 will be *₹233241*.

Let's now view the difference in both the Scenarios through Bar graph plotting: -

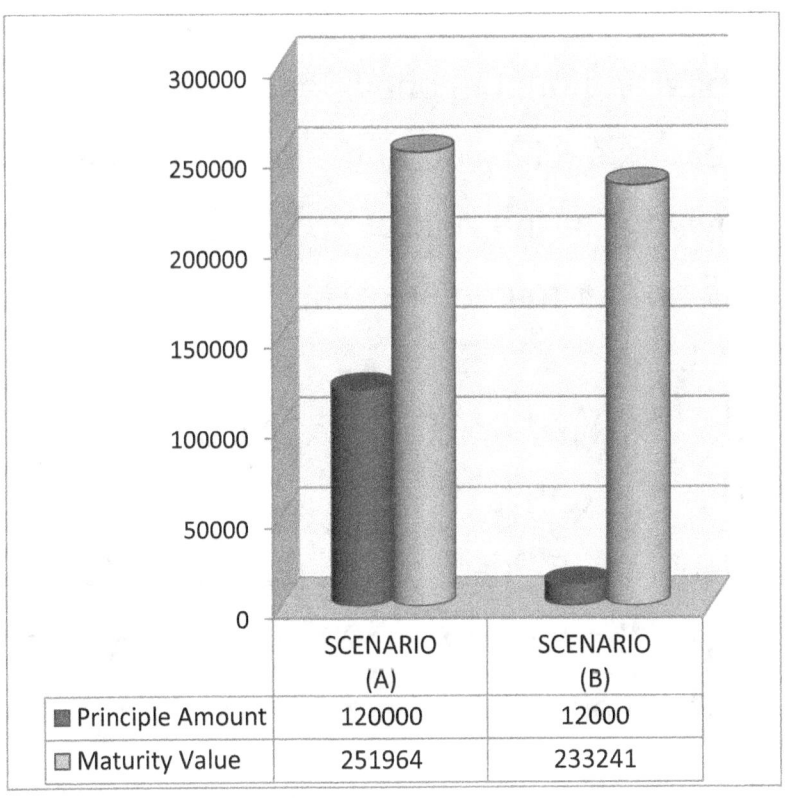

If we compare these two Scenarios then we can see that the final corpus of SCENARIO – A is larger than the SCENARIO – B but if we compare the growth then it is clearly observed that in SCENARIO – A the Maturity value is 2× and in SCENARIO – B the final corpus is *19.43x* of the Principal Amount.

Let's take **SCENARIO – (C)** in which the Person is 18yro and he/she saves ₹200 per day as pocket money and keeps collecting that money for 2 years which becomes ₹120000 and then he decides to invest it at the age of 20 till the age of 60 for his/her retirement.

So, Principal Amount - ₹120000
N.S.C. (ROI) – 7.7%
Tenure – 5 years (up to 60 years of age). Here the person is 20, so 8 times the investment will be done.

C.I. - ₹120000 × $(1+7.7\%)^5$ = ₹173884. (1$^{st}$)

In next 5 years, it will be –
C.I. - ₹173884 × $(1+7.7\%)^5$ = ₹251964 (2$^{nd}$)
In next 5 years, it will be –
C.I. - ₹251964 × $(1+7.7\%)^5$ = ₹365104 (3$^{rd}$)

In next 5 years, it will be –

C.I. - ₹365104 × $(1+7.7\%)^5$ = ₹529048 (4th)

In next 5 years, it will be –

C.I. - ₹529048 × $(1+7.7\%)^5$ = ₹766608 (5th)

In next 5 years, it will be –

C.I. - ₹766608 × $(1+7.7\%)^5$ = ₹1110841 (6th)

In next 5 years, it will be – (7th)

C.I. - ₹1110841 × $(1+7.7\%)^5$ = ₹1609646

In next 5 years, it will be – (8th)

C.I. - ₹1609646 × $(1+7.7\%)^5$ = ₹2332431

Thus, the maturity value at the age of 60 will be **₹2332431**.

Let's evaluate the three Scenarios in Bar graph plotted bellow –

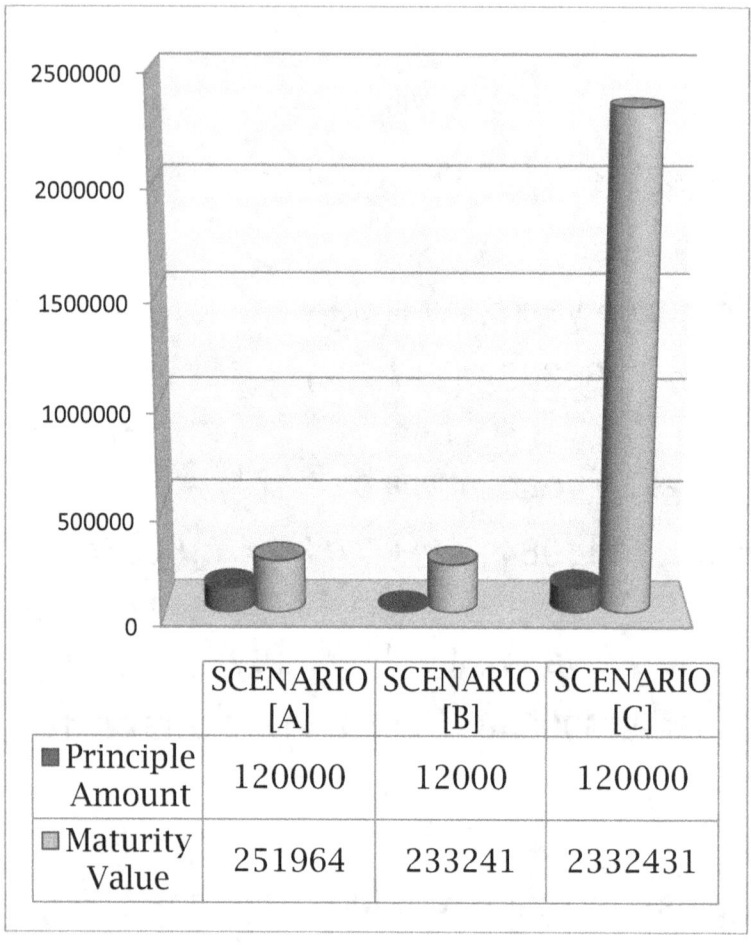

|  | SCENARIO [A] | SCENARIO [B] | SCENARIO [C] |
|---|---|---|---|
| ■ Principle Amount | 120000 | 12000 | 120000 |
| ■ Maturity Value | 251964 | 233241 | 2332431 |

If we closely observe the difference then, it is clearly seen that the Growth on Investment in each Scenarios as per its Principal Amount is in a sequence of **SCENARIO – A<B<C!**

Another type of Investment is also known as K.V.P (Kisan Vikas Patra) which is another famous savings method offered by Post Office similar to that of N.S.C but has long duration of time with 7.5% interest rate (as of F.Y 23-24) compounded annually and has a tenure of 10yrs 4months or 124 months.

It can be opened by an Adult (18yrs of age and above) or of a minor above 10yrs separately and bellow 10yrs of age can be opened with a guardian. Joint Accounts can also be opened with up to 3 adults.

Considering the previous Scenarios we will again calculate it for K.V.P.

Here, Tenure – 10yrs and 4 months
And, ROI% - 7.5% annually
Or, 7.5÷12 = 0.625% monthly

For **SCENARIO – A**, it will be –
C.I. – ₹120000× $(1+0.625\%)^{124}$ = **₹253507**

For **SCENARIO – B**, it will be – (1$^{st}$)
C.I. – ₹12000× $(1+0.625\%)^{124}$ = ₹25351

In next 10 years it will be – (2ⁿᵈ)
C.I. – ₹25351× (1+0.625%) ¹²⁴ = ₹53555

In next 10 years it will be – (3ʳᵈ)
C.I. – ₹53555× (1+0.625%) ¹²⁴ = ₹113138

In next 10 years it will be – (4ᵗʰ)
C.I. – ₹113138× (1+0.625%) ¹²⁴ = **₹239011**

For **SCENARIO – C**, it will be – (1ˢᵗ)
C.I. – ₹120000× (1+0.625%) ¹²⁴ = ₹253507

In next 10 years it will be – (2ⁿᵈ)
C.I. – ₹253507× (1+0.625%) ¹²⁴ = ₹535548

In next 10 years it will be – (3ʳᵈ)
C.I. – ₹535548× (1+0.625%) ¹²⁴ = ₹1131376

In next 10 years it will be – (4ᵗʰ)
C.I. – ₹1131376× (1+0.625%) ¹²⁴ = **₹2390097**

Therefore it is clear that whatever the case may be, if you start early with a small amount you may accumulate a lot in long term whereas if you start late then, you may have to struggle through savings.

# Goal Planning

*"A Goal without a Plan is just a Dream which might not come true!"*

The above Statement is true to each and every context of life but if we concentrate on the Finance perspective, then we will get to know in this chapter about its importance and consequences of not planning future goals from a practical and logical point of view.

As discussed in the previous chapter, just have a look at the Bar graph plotted on Page 38 which clearly shows the drastic effect of starting early vs. being late irrespective of the money invested.

Now the question arises that for what purpose we need to save or invest the money because if there's no Goal to it then you might end up saving and investing for your entire life and will never be able to achieve something rather at the end moments of your life you may have regret of whatever you saved, as they were no use to you. We have this beautiful life with us which needs to be planned earlier as it's said that *"Being prepared at present is better than having regret in future."*

There can be various Goals in one's life as they can depend on your desires/wants based on the superior lifestyle in comparison to that of the present. But if we concentrate on a broader perspective then they can be classified in needs and common wants/desires of a middle class family.

There are various calculations done while planning each Goal, try to evaluate your own Goals by using the formulas and have a check on your future planning!!

In a decreasing order of requirement, the various goals are as follows:–

1. **Emergency Fund** –

    This is the most important Goal one needs to start compulsorily as soon as he/she starts earning as it is a fund needed while an emergency and needs to be kept aside i.e., should never be used in casual spending for anything irrespective of that goods/service be an asset or a liability. This fund should be completely restricted to withdrawal at the time of any unfortunate incidents or crisis if takes place for avoiding the financial crisis at those times.

    The simple rule says that you should have at least a fund saved of 6 months or better to be of 1 year of your salary. As this fund needs to be stable, so the best way is to create a Recurring

Deposit (R.D) in your Bank of 10% of your monthly salary for a period of 55-60 months and then create a Fixed Deposit (F.D) of the Maturity value accumulated from that Recurring Deposit (R.D) and in this way you will accumulate your Corpus of Emergency Fund within 5 Years of being employed.

2. **Retirement Planning –**

The most important future planning yet ignored by many people, it is a very common myth believed by many of us that as our E.P.F and N.P.S is being deducted from the salary is itself enough to bear all the future expenses after we retire. Sadly, that's not the truth as future is completely unpredictable and expenses at that time might increase due to several factors in which the additional expense added will be routine medical checkups and full-time maid service for all the day to day needs of a person at his/her old age. We should always have additional investments in which the employers having E.P.F (if not then opt for P.P.F) and N.P.S can opt for retirement planning solution oriented investment funds (See Pg. – 144-152).

3. **Marriage Expense** –

In India, the biggest Celebration in one's life is their Wedding and mostly the biggest Expense of one's life, in foreign Countries it is also recognized as 'The Big Fat Indian Wedding'. Majority of the people in India get married within few years of being in a stable job/business. Now in the initial years of earnings we don't bother caring much about the upcoming expenses which creates a problem in future to the unavoidable expenses. Considering Weddings in India of a Middle Class Family, it varies in a range from ₹500000 - ₹5000000 depending upon being lower/upper middle class. This range gives us an average of ₹2000000 - ₹2500000 which is a big amount of money needed to be spent on a single occasion and needs to be pre-planned accordingly.

If I assume the age of a person with a stable income to be 27-30 then even if he gets married at the age of 32-35 has 5 years of time period to accumulate the money for it. This is a moderate time period which means we can't fully rely on returns generated by savings scheme and thus we need to add Equity (Stock Market) returns to it and the safest option to invest in Stock Market is to invest via Mutual Fund. In my opinion (need not to be blindly followed as Volatility in returns are subject to market risk) a person can invest 30-40%% of his/her monthly salary for the accumulation of Marriage Expense as at that period of time being single will not have much monthly expense and thus can be adjusted in 50-60% of the monthly salary.

Let us take an Example of a person of 28 years of age having a monthly in hand salary of ₹40000 wants to get married at the age of 33 is already saving 10% of the monthly salary for his Emergency Fund which is ₹4000 and wants to save 35% of salary which is ₹14000. Thus, 10+35%=45% being saved and 55% left for monthly expense which will be ₹22000 and it is a considerable amount of money to live alone with your own expenses before getting married. Now, the amount being saved for the Emergency Fund will only continue for 1 year post which the person may continue with the amount being already invested or may increase it by adding 10% post 1 year to increase the amount of the corpus needed to be accumulated within 5 years. So if the person chooses to increase the investment by 10% then post 1 year it will become 10+35%=45% of ₹40000 which is ₹4000+₹14000=₹18000/month. Now if we split the amount being saved for the Wedding Expense then, 60% should be Recurring Deposit (R.D) and remaining 40% in Mutual Fund (we will discuss about it in upcoming chapters) in a systematic manner also known as

SIP (Systematic Investment Plan). As far as the returns are concerned then, we know that R.D provides a fixed rate of return on maximum of 8% (varies) whereas, returns of the Mutual Funds varies a lot but gives an average of 12% (not assured, may be lower or higher as said earlier it varies a lot) of returns mostly if invested for a long period of time.

For the 1$^{st}$ Year, the investment will be 35% of ₹40000 which is ₹14000 and 60% of ₹14000 which is ₹8900 or ₹9000/month in R.D and 40% of ₹14000 which is ₹5100 or ₹5000/month of S.I.P in a Mutual Fund.

So in R.D, it will be –

$M = R [(1+i)^n - 1] \div [1-(1+i)^{-1/3}]$

Where, (M) = RD maturity value

(R) = Monthly installment

(n) = Number of quarters

(i) = Interest rate/400

So here according to the assumptions,

It will be –

(R) = ₹9,000

(n) = 4 (4 quarters in a year)

(i) = 8÷400

Thus, $M = R[(1+i)^n - 1] \div [1-(1+i)^{-1/3}]$

$M = 9000[(1+8\div400)^4 - 1] \div [1-(1+8\div400)^{-1/3}]$

= **₹112763.**

In S.I.P it will be –

$F.V = P[(1+i)^n - 1] \times (1+i)/i$

Where,

F.V = Future Value

P = Amount you invest through S.I.P

i = Compounded rate of return

n = Investment duration in months

r = expected rate of return

Here,

(r) = 12%

(P) = ₹5000

(n) = 12

(i) = r/n = 12%/12 (12= months in a year) = 0.01.

F.V = 5000 [$(1+0.01)^{12}-1$] × (1+0.01)/0.01 = **₹64047**

So, Maturity Value of R.D is ₹112763 + Maturity Value of S.I.P is ₹64047 = **₹176810** which can be invested for 4 years in Lump sum Mutual Fund which is similar to F.D in Stock Market and as linked to the Market it is also volatile.

Now, Lump sum investment in Mutual Fund will be – FV = PV $(1+r)^n$

Where,

FV = Future value
PV = Present Value
r = rate of interest
n = number of years
Here, PV = ₹176810, r = 12%, n = 4
So, ₹176810 $(1+12\%)^4$ = **₹278214**... (I)

For the next 4 Years, the investment will be 45% of ₹40000 which is ₹18000 and 60% of ₹18000 which is ₹10800 or ₹11000/month in R.D and 40% of ₹18000 which is ₹7200 or ₹7000/month of S.I.P in a Mutual Fund.

So in R.D, it will be –

$M = R [(1+i)^n - 1] \div [1-(1+i)^{-1/3}]$

Where, (M) = RD maturity value

(R) = Monthly installment

(n) = Number of quarters

(i) = Interest rate/400

So here, according to the assumptions it will be –

(R) = ₹4,000

(n) = 16 (4 quarters in a year)

(i) = 8÷400

Thus, $M = R [(1+i)^n - 1] \div [1-(1+i)^{-1/3}]$

$M = 11000[(1+8\div 400)^{16} - 1] \div [1-(1+8\div 400)^{-1/3}]$

= **₹623280….. (ii)**

In S.I.P it will be –

$$F.V = P [(1+i)^n - 1] \times (1+i)/i$$

Where,

F.V = Future Value

P = Amount you invest through S.I.P

i = Compounded rate of return

n = Investment duration in months

r = expected rate of return

Here,

(r) = 12%

(P) = ₹7000

(n) = 48

(i) = r/n = 12%/12 (12 = months in a year) = 0.01.

$$F.V = 7000 [(1+0.01)^{48} - 1] \times (1+0.01)/0.01 =$$ **₹432844….. (iii)**

So, Total Amount accumulated in 5 years for Wedding Expense [(i) + (ii) + (iii)] is –

₹278214 + ₹623280 + ₹432844 = **₹1334338.**

The Amount is less than the estimated average Wedding Expense which is around ₹2000000 - ₹2500000. It can also be achieved by the same method just by reversing the equation of 60% in Mutual Funds and 40% in Recurring Deposit (try it yourself). But if both the partners are working and their families are financially stable then as because Marriage is a symbol of a Relationship with equal rights and promises to share each aspect of our life, equally we should also allow the Marriage Expense to be equally pulled up by both Bride and Bridegroom and if done, then the entire equation done earlier fits best for both individually.

After getting married and having a Baby one should definitely subscribe to a Medical/Health Insurance about which we will discuss in later chapters.

## 4. Child Education –

Soon after getting married in our example it was at an age of 33 you will have a baby within 1 or 2 years and as after the birth of your baby your life will surround across the upbringing of your child which will make you procrastinate the future planning of the child as it may seem silly but as you get busy in your daily life routines time will flow like sand from your hand. It is better to plan it within a year of being married. Every child is unique and underlies a lot of talent within themselves which can definitely not be planned earlier but apart from upbringing of the child we can plan his/her future expenses if required in future which is majorly Higher Education of your child or anything else.

For example, you are planning for any future expense of your Child required at the age of 18 then you can allocate 20% of your net monthly in hand salary for next 18 years and as the time frame is large thus, investing the entire money in Mutual Funds through S.I.P will be more beneficial than continuing in traditional savings method.

The volatility can be adjusted by exiting from the Mutual Fund few years back and investing the maturity amount in traditional savings schemes to get stable returns yet beating the inflation across the time.

It is highly recommended to try calculating the maturity value of your child's future expense by your own with the help of the previous examples.

## 5. Owning a House –

In India, decision of owning a house and its expense is perhaps the biggest decision of one's life. Most of the people who get recently married either live with their parents as a joint family in their own house or live separately as P.G (Paying Guest) at another place due to job location being far from the hometown or any other reason for that matter. Nowadays, as the nuclear families are increasing the problem to own a house is very predominant among us and it has various reasons as P.G has certain limitations and moreover if the job is transferable (which is most likely) then shifting of the household items becomes a headache and thus we ignore having large items which certainly hampers the living standard even after being financially able to buy the goods and accessories. If one has the luxury of having a non-transferable stable job in the hometown then this is a blessing to them but as most of the people do not fall under that category hence, we need to plan our purchasing of a new accommodation for living.

Whenever we talk about buying a new house, Home Loan is the most lucrative option we find for and even Banks sell them as the one and only option of buying a new house as gaining such a huge amount would not be possible if loan is not availed from the Banks. In context of a middle class family, to some extent it's true but not entirely as because a new house can range from ₹1500000 to ₹5000000 depending on district areas to metro city respectively. If we take an average value of owning a house in India then it will be easily in the range of ₹2500000 to ₹3000000 which if taken a Home Loan will charge an average interest rate of 9% (as of 2023 by taking average of all top banks providing home loans in India) and due to compounding the more the tenure of the Loan will be the higher the interest will be accumulated by the banks and that's the reason why banks sell Loans of high tenure as it provides greater interest to Banks due to compounding and the borrower also has to give less money on the monthly basis. If we evaluate the relation between them then it comes out to be as –

Loan Tenure $\propto$ Interest Accumulated

Loan Tenure $\propto \dfrac{1}{\text{EMI per Month}}$

So here develops two scenarios, one is that the person is quite comfortable with his/her present lifestyle and wants to have a dream home later on.

While the second one can be a bit desperate to shift in a new home as soon as possible because of being fed up of the tantrums of P.G. (Paying Guest) and for both of them the planning to own a house will be different.

So, let us have a look in both of these scenarios: –

**SCENARIO – I:** A person with a stable job and a happy family at the age of 30 earning in hand salary of ₹40000/month wants to have a dream house worth ₹3000000 in the next 10-12 years of time period.

Now, he is already investing 20% of his salary for the child's future expenses.

In this scenario the person should plan to start investing money to accumulate the corpus required for buying the house after 12 years.

So, assuming the person has a monthly expense of ₹24000 which is 60% of his/her monthly salary and ₹8000 being invested in child's future which is 20% of the monthly income, now he/she has 20% left for investing to buy a house but if we can adjust the monthly expense by just ₹2000 then it will become 55% and we will have 25% of monthly salary for investing to buy a house which becomes ₹10000.

We can invest this amount through S.I.P in mutual Funds as discussed about it earlier, which will be –

$F.V = P [(1+i)^n - 1] \times (1+i)/i$

Where,

F.V = Future Value

P = Amount you invest through S.I.P

i = Compounded rate of return

n = Investment duration in months

r = expected rate of return

Here,

(r) = 12%

(P) = ₹10000,

(n) = 144

(i) = r/12 (12 = no. of months in a year) = 12%/12 = 0.01.

$F.V = 10000[(1+0.01)^{144} - 1] \times (1+0.01)/0.01$

= **₹3222522**

Now even if the Maturity amount seems to be a bit higher than the amount required, a great factor 'inflation' is missing in it which is responsible for the increase in price of goods and services over a period of time.

As inflation will cost the sum of ₹3000000 to be – $FV = PV(1+r)^n$

Where,

FV = Future value

PV = Present Value = ₹3000000

r = rate of inflation = 4% (retail inflation in 2023)

n = number of years = 12

So, $F.V = ₹3000000 (1+4\%)^{12}$

**= ₹4803097.**

Thus after 12 years, the cost of owning a house will become expensive from that of the present value. Now, if we look at our investment's Maturity value then it is lesser in comparison to the amount required while purchasing the house after 12 years of time period. As we have already added 5% to the monthly investment by cutting down 5% from the monthly expense, now we cannot cut our monthly expenses further but there's a way which is the yearly increment in the salary which happens every single year to any salaried class. This increment is usually about 10%/year, now if we take advantage of this and instead of keeping it in the bank account we can start our Step-up S.I.P which is S.I.P with an increment in it as per the frequency set by the investor. So, we can add 10% increment of the salary to the S.I.P in the form of Step-up/Top-up S.I.P.

Let's calculate the maturity value if monthly investment or S.I.P is increased or Top-up by 10% per year for 12 years.

In the 1$^{st}$ Year of Step up S.I.P will be –

F.V=10000[(1+0.01) $^{12}$-1] × (1+0.01)/0.01
= **₹128093**

In the 2$^{nd}$ Year of Step up S.I.P will be –

F.V=11000[(1+0.01) $^{12}$-1] × (1+0.01)/0.01
+ ₹128093 (1+0.01)$^{12}$ = **₹285241**

In the 3$^{rd}$ Year of Step up S.I.P will be –

F.V=12100[(1+0.01) $^{12}$-1] × (1+0.01)/0.01
+ ₹285241 (1+0.01)$^{12}$ = **₹476410**

In the 4$^{th}$ Year of Step up S.I.P will be –

F.V=13310[(1+0.01) $^{12}$-1] × (1+0.01)/0.01
+ ₹476410 (1+0.01)$^{12}$ = **₹707323**

In the 5$^{th}$ Year of Step up S.I.P will be –

F.V=14641[(1+0.01) $^{12}$-1] × (1+0.01)/0.01
+ ₹707323 (1+0.01)$^{12}$ = **₹984571**

In the 6$^{th}$ Year of Step up S.I.P will be –

F.V=16105[(1+0.01)$^{12}$-1] × (1+0.01)/0.01 + ₹984571 (1+0.01)$^{12}$ = **₹1315733**

In the 7$^{th}$ Year of Step up S.I.P will be –

F.V=17716[(1+0.01)$^{12}$-1] × (1+0.01)/0.01 + ₹1315733 (1+0.01)$^{12}$ = **₹1709531**

In the 8$^{th}$ Year of Step up S.I.P will be –

F.V=19487[(1+0.01)$^{12}$-1] × (1+0.01)/0.01 + ₹1709531 (1+0.01)$^{12}$ = **₹2175958**

In the 9$^{th}$ Year of Step up S.I.P will be –

F.V=21436[(1+0.01)$^{12}$-1] × (1+0.01)/0.01 + ₹2175958 (1+0.01)$^{12}$ = **₹2726505**

In the 10$^{th}$ Year of Step up S.I.P will be –

F.V=23580[(1+0.01)$^{12}$-1] × (1+0.01)/0.01 + ₹2726505 (1+0.01)$^{12}$ = **₹3374338**

In the 11$^{th}$ Year of Step up S.I.P will be –

F.V=25938[(1+0.01)$^{12}$-1] × (1+0.01)/0.01 + ₹3374338 (1+0.01)$^{12}$ = **₹4134537**

In the 12$^{th}$ Year of Step up S.I.P will be –

F.V=28532[(1+0.01)$^{12}$-1] × (1+0.01)/0.01 + ₹4134537 (1+0.01)$^{12}$ = **₹5024376**

Therefore, now we have a Maturity Amount of ₹5024376 whereas, the inflation adjusted cost required to purchase the house was ₹4803097 which creates an extra difference of **₹5024376-₹4803097 = ₹221279**.

This shows us that even in the lesser time, if we remain disciplined though our investments then we can get the desired amount as the Maturity Value.

**SCENARIO – II:** A person with a stable job and a happy family at the age of 42 earning in hand salary of ₹100000 per month wants to immediately shift in a house worth ₹3000000 and has a monthly expense of 45% of the salary and is already investing 25% of his salary for the child's expenses which means 30% of the salary is saved which is ₹30000 per month.

In this scenario the person has no time to plan and invest to buy a house; rather he/she has the only option to take a Home Loan from a Bank. But, even here emerges two cases in which if the person select for a plan to keep the Loan for shorter duration which will cost high E.M.I but saves the Interest paid during the Loan tenure or the person select for a plan of longer duration which will cost low E.M.I but will accumulate high interest during the loan tenure.

Let's explore both the Cases –

<u>CASE – I</u>: The person chooses to get a home loan of ₹3000000 at an interest rate of 9%/annum for a tenure of 20 years.

Now, to calculate the E.M.I of the Loan a formula is used as –

$$E = [P \times R \times (1+R)^N] \div [(1+R)^N - 1]$$

Where,

E = E.M.I Amount

P = Principal Amount

R = Rate of Interest in months

N = Loan Tenure in months

$$E = [3000000 \times 0.75\% \times (1+0.75\%)^{240}] \div [(1+0.75\%)^{240} - 1] = ₹26992$$

Now, Interest Accumulated can be obtained by: (E.M.I×N) – P

(₹26992×240) - ₹3000000 = **₹3478080**

<u>CASE – II</u>: The person chooses to get a home loan of ₹3000000 at an interest rate of 9%/annum for a tenure of 15 years.

Now, to calculate the E.M.I of the Loan a formula is used as –

$$E = [P \times R \times (1+R)^N] \div [(1+R)^N - 1]$$

Where,

E = E.M.I Amount
P = Principal Amount
R = Rate of Interest in months
N = Loan Tenure in months

$$E = [3000000 \times 0.75\% \times (1+0.75\%)^{180}] \div [(1+0.75\%)^{180} - 1] = ₹30428$$

Now, Interest Accumulated can be obtained by: (E.M.I×N) - P

(₹30428×180) - ₹3000000 = **₹2477040**

It can be clearly seen that the E.M.I of (CASE – I) < (CASE – II) whereas, the Interest Accumulated in the tenure will be (CASE – I) > (CASE – II). If we compare the E.M.I of both the Cases then it will be - ₹30428-₹26992 = **₹3436** whereas, the difference between the Interest Accumulated in the tenure is ₹3478080-₹2477040 = **₹1001040**

## 6. Travel Expense –

Travelling is not just a way of refreshing and entertaining yourself but also a way to explore the diversity among different cultures, food, languages, and lot more. But, to Travel to new places exploring different things domestically or across the international borders requires a plan which needs to be detailed and a budget including every possible estimated expense. Ideally, if you are planning for a vacation it should be planned much before the actual vacation to take place and after having an estimated budget you can opt for a simple R.D (Recurring

Deposit) in which the monthly installment will be $\frac{Estimated\ Budget}{Months\ left\ for\ vaccation}$ as if the Budget is ₹100000 and Months left for vacation is 8 months then, R.D installment = $\frac{₹100000}{8}$ = ₹12500/month.

7. **Owning a Car** –

Owning a car might be an ease of transportation but now-a-days it is more of a symbol of status in the society as the fancy and luxurious your car the more you are supposed to be rich, but the reality may hit hard as just because of the fake status symbol people tend to buy expensive cars which are beyond their budget by purchasing through unsecured debts and get trapped within the 'debt trap'. To avoid that and fulfill the desire of purchasing the dream car, banks came up with Car loan.

These loans charge an average interest rate of 9.5%p.a in the range of 8%p.a – 11%p.a which are compounded and calculated on a monthly basis.

Example – A person aged 32 years earning ₹50000/month wants to buy a Car worth ₹800000 seeks loan from the Bank offering the loan amount at an interest rate of 9%p.a (compounded monthly) for a tenure of 5 years.

Now, to calculate the E.M.I of the Loan a formula is used as –

$$E = [P \times R \times (1+R)^N] \div [(1+R)^N - 1]$$

Where,

E = E.M.I Amount
P = Principal Amount
R = Rate of Interest in months
N = Loan Tenure in months

$$E = [800000 \times 0.75\% \times (1+0.75\%)^{60}] \div [(1+0.75\%)^{60} - 1] = ₹16607$$

Now, Interest Accumulated can be obtained by: (E.M.I×N) - P

(₹16607×60) - ₹800000 = **₹196420.**

So, if you have time it's always better to plan a car few years before purchasing it and save the money through R.D as monthly installments instead of E.M.I as loan.

Besides planning for a Car emotionally it is always recommended to analyze the need of the Car practically because Car is said to be 'Depreciating Asset' as the Car loses its value with time and comes along with many expenses such as fuel, maintenance, etc. The moment a person buys a Car, it becomes a second hand Car and thus the price of the Car decreases drastically apart of it being used by the owner.

In Urban/Rural areas most of the places have Cabs/Taxis easily accessible and can be used as an alternative to owning a Car if you have *less outing*, as because a Taxi fare booked in lifetime will always be lesser than the cost of owning a Car!

# Risk Profile Assessment

*"Risk always exists as an outcome of a decision which is evaluated by its Opportunity Cost!"*

The above statement simply means that whenever you decide to take an action, at that very moment a 'Risk' is also involved in it which may be avoided/reduced if the decision taken involves analysis of possible outcomes and measurement of Risk to Reward Ratio as per the person's Risk Appetite.

In the World of Finance, A statement is very popular which says –

"Higher is the Risk; higher is the Returns and vice-versa."

According to the statement, $Risk \propto Returns$. To some extent it is true, but that doesn't mean we start to invest our money in the Risky Instruments.

As, Risk in terms of Investment simply means volatility in the Returns generated on a corpus.

Apart from all the statements mentioned, if a Person takes a decision without knowing the process of its outcome then he/she will surely make a Loss in terms of Investment. The Incomplete knowledge is far more dangerous than having no knowledge about an Investing instrument in Finance.

There are several stages of life and accordingly we need to plan our Investments through which we can be prepared for the Future with maximum Growth and minimum Risk.

The stages of life are mainly –

1. **Childhood (<10yrs)** – Here, the Person is totally dependent on their parents or indirectly we can say financially unaware as an individual.

2. **Adolescence (10-18yrs)** – This is the stage where the person encounters with the use of money for the first time by understanding its importance through spending it in a Shop or by saving it in the form of Pocket Money.

3. **Adulthood** – It also has three sub-categories as Young Adults, Matured Adults and Retired Adults.

   (a) *Young Adults (18-28yrs)* –
   They are quite similar to those in Adolescence; the only difference is that they are now being gradually prepared to become independent from the dependency of their parents in terms of money. Thus, it is a transition phase.

   (b) *Matured Adults (28-60yrs)* –
   These are the people who have steady growth in their earnings through a Job or a Business and are planning to settle down with Family. This is the largest phase in anyone's life.

   (c) *Retired Adults (60-70yrs)* –
   This is the phase when a Person (if planned his/her life properly) enjoys the freedom of life because of being Financially Independent, but it also

depends on the various circumstances and thus very few people enjoy this phase of life and rest of them remain in a regret of circumstances or mistakes made earlier in their life.

4. **Old Age (70-85yrs)** – These are the People who are the most vulnerable to health and diseases, they need a fulltime assistance for their day-day activities, they are now least bothered about money and want their legal heir to take care of it. This is the last stage of one's life.

Many of us think that according to the above mentioned stages of life, the Financial Planning should get started from the stage of 'Matured Adults' but that's the most common mistake anyone does, because at that time you are planning to settle down in life which means you are now ready to take responsibilities of your family. But, if you start planning now then do you already have Emergency Fund, Insurance and other Assets required at the time of emergency? If not then you are still dependent on our Parents, Friends, Family, etc. which can create a drastic imbalance of money flow or even worst you may get into a money cycle trap.

The right age is the stage of 'Adolescence' because when you start a Financial Planning then the most important thing is to understand the nature of money and your relation with money which gradually increases as we spend more time in learning about it. It is a wrong belief that if Adolescents are taught about money then they will become addicted to it, but that's not true. If you observe yourself or an Adolescent in your family then you will find that parents always avoid to talk about money and all our understandings and beliefs takes place from the friends who are also an Adolescent which creates a fixed pattern to use the money.

Everyone has a set of beliefs to which they follow blindly without knowing its outcomes or future consequences. As someone develops a nature to spend money without keeping its records as they find it useless whereas someone who does that are called as a money bug in his/her friend circle.

In this situation, it is the duty of the Guardian to observe and clarify the doubts of their child as the beliefs/tendency which once get created in Adolescence lasts for the entire life and are very hard to change in future.

Money isn't a bad thing, it just needs to be understood properly so that we can plan and prepare our life expenses which are definite or indefinite in future.

Now we will evaluate the various kinds of Risk involved in every stage of life. As every stage has its own Risk, so we will point it out in an order as follows –

As discussed earlier, we will start it with Adolescent stage and then gradually move towards the Old Age.

1. **Adolescent Stage** – This is the phase where the Money is introduced to us for the first time, so the Risk involved is of

'Wrong perception about Money' and once it's created can't be changed easily in future.

2. **Young Adult Stage** – It is a crucial phase of life and the Risk involved here is *'FOMO (Fear of Missing Out)'* as everyone has done something means it is right and thus I should also do it, eventually will only leave regret after taking any decision.

3. **Matured Adults** – This is the most important phase of everyone's life, at this point the biggest Risk is *'Considering there's enough time to think about Money, I will plan it latter.'* This one statement has left regrets to >90% of the Population under this age group.

4. **Retired Adults** – This is the phase when your disciplined Budgeting and Planning at your earlier stage of life rewards you. The Risk involved in this phase is *'Regret of Past and shortage of Money due to unplanned uncertain expenses'*. The harsh Reality of our Society and then we blame our fate.

5. **Old Age** – At this stage, most of the people are done with their life. It is the time to be Happy and Satisfied from the journey of life. The biggest mistake/Risk involved here is *'To be completely unaware of your Money and Assets or to give control of your Finances to unworthy person'*. The entire Old Age Homes are mostly filled with the Old Age people who were thrown out of their homes after getting access over Money and other Assets.

Well, it's important to be aware of your Risk but it is more important to accept it and implement the solutions for better financial future.


Solutions for each stage is discussed bellow –

- **Adolescent Stage** – 'Wrong perception about Money.' It can be only changed by understanding the importance and role of Money in day-day life. By exploring the relationship with Money.

- **Young Adults** – The *'FOMO (Fear of Missing Out).'* It can be mitigated by Patience, because this is the problem of restlessness for not being indulged in an activity which is very popular regardless of its outcomes, need or relevance in one's life. It also needs to be cross-verified through own research before getting into it.
- **Matured Adults** – *'Considering there's enough time to think about Money, I will plan it latter.'* It is the problem of not realizing the importance of Planning and Budgeting as it feels very boring, they tend to ignore their future expenses. The only solution to this is take a Weekend off, sit with the family and start a conversation on what's needed in next few years, you will surely get an idea of the expense and then try to evaluate it with your today's financial condition. Does it matches perfectly or there's a mismatch/shortcoming? I'm sure you will be shocked and if yes then please start planning your future expenses as soon as possible.

- **_Retired Adults_** – *'Regret of Past and shortage of Money due to unplanned uncertain expenses.'* Always remember that it's never too late and every problem has a solution. If you are stuck in such a situation, then try to seek help from your known one's or better consult a Finance Advisor. The solution to the problems won't be easy but it is better to find a way instead of losing hope.
- **_Old Age_** - *'To be completely unaware of your Money and Assets or to give control of your Finances to unworthy person'*. Most of the people at this stage become very careless about their own and are least bothered about their surroundings. It is very important to understand that they are still alive and they need at least basic requirements of human life with a lot of care and affection.

It is important to decide/plan about everything earlier and choose a person who is committed selflessly, so that everything else gets taken care of by him/her.

Now, after covering solutions to every problem we will try to understand the broader perspective of relation between Time, Risk and Money. As it is said that –

$$\text{"Time} \propto \text{Risk} \propto \text{Wealth"}$$

It simply means that – More the Time invested, higher the Risk can be taken and Higher the Risk taken will generate large corpus of Wealth along with the time.

Another famous equation says –

$$\text{"Risk\% = 100 – Age"}$$

It simply calculates the amount of Risk needed to be taken for better Return on Investments, because Risk in Investments causes volatility which can be beneficial in long term investing methods.

Following the two equations mentioned we could generate different results for each life stages. But we will start from the stage of Matured Adults as before that a person may not have his/her own source of income or stability within the income source. It is also important to understand the right Age from which we can start planning for the future in a systematic manner, taking adequate Risk as and when required. Stages earlier to this should be focused on understanding and building a strong relationship with Money.

Now, we will analyze the Risk Appetite of each Life Stages as follows –

1. **Matured Adult Stage** –

    - The Minimum Age of a person remains around 28, so the Risk Appetite as per the formula will be *Risk% = 100 – 28 = 72%*

    - The Average Age of a person is 44 (in between 28 - 60) so the Risk Appetite can be calculated as *Risk% = 100 – 44 = 56%*

    - The Maximum Age is 60, so the Risk Appetite will be calculated as *Risk% = 100 – 60 = 40%*

So it simply indicates that –

At the Initial stage of Matured Adults, they can invest 72% in Risky Assets (volatile returns) whereas; the remaining 28% can be Fixed Assets.

At the Mid-Stage of Matured Adults, they can invest 56% in Risky Assets (volatile returns) whereas; the remaining 44% can be invested in Fixed Assets.

At the Last-Stage of Matured Adults, they can invest 40% in Risky Assets (volatile returns) whereas; the remaining 60% can be invested in Fixed Assets.

| MATURED ADULTS | RISKY ASSETS | FIXED ASSETS |
|---|---|---|
| Minimum Age | 72% | 28% |
| Average Age | 56% | 44% |
| Maximum Age | 40% | 60% |

## 2. Retired Adult Stage –

If a person has followed the investment pattern required for Matured Adults then they will surely accumulate enough Wealth to live life in their own way being Financially Independent and if a person had build up the habit of savings from their Adolescent period then it will work as a cherry on the cake. But, as we all know that implementation is the key and if not been disciplined in it then it is of no use as because **"Compounding is initially slow but gives fastest growth at final stage."**

If you failed to remain disciplined, then you may repeat the process of calculating Risk% as per your age for next 10 years.

## 3. Old Age –

At this stage, keep all your Money in Fixed Assets which are very liquid (easily available to withdraw), try to keep record on your transactions as far as possible and if can't then hand over this responsibility to a wise and honest person (need not to be compulsorily a family member), just the one you Trust.

# Insure Your Future

*"Life is uncertain, but Death isn't!"*

Life is full of uncertainty, every event which may occur in future has a possibility but Health problems and Death are certain and thus needs to be insured.

Insurance is a financial protection against Person/Assets which provides a sum assured to the beneficiary due to the loss occurred to the Person/Assets.

In our society, Insurance is the most under-rated financial instrument and the reason behind this is the misconception about the purpose of having Insurance. As in most of the cases it is often seen that people tend to have Insurance to reduce the tax liability and consider it as an investment which will additionally generate some returns along with the protection which is provided through the Insurance.

But, they do not understand that nothing comes free of cost. If any Insurance scheme provides assured returns over the period of Insurance along with the protection then it simply means that the money will be invested in an asset/financial instrument which will generate a return on the corpus providing lesser protection amount as it would have been without any return on investment.

We need to understand that Insurance and Investment are two purely different aspects of finance. Investments are done to accumulate wealth for our needs and desires whereas Insurance is done to protect our depreciating assets/ourselves and family from emergency which may occur in anyone's life.

There are various types of insurance available in the market but some of the most important are –

1. **Life/Term Insurance** –

    It is one of the most important yet mostly ignored Insurance, because it provides financial support to your dependents/family members when you die unfortunately before the time period of Insurance cover. Nowadays due to rush lifestyle, being alive healthy for a long period of time has became quite difficult and possibilities of early death are also arising at an alarming rate which creates an immense need of having a Term life Insurance.

Let's understand some of the basic components of a Life/Health Insurance.

A Life/Health Insurance depends upon multiple factors associated with the lifestyle of a person being insured which are discussed as follows –

- **Age** – The Person's age matters the most because a Term Insurance Plan will always depend upon the tenure of lifespan which gets insured of a person. If a person gets the Term Insurance at an early age then he/she will have to pay lesser premiums on the Capital insured in comparison to the one who gets it later on for the same corpus insured.

- **Lifestyle & Diseases** – It is the second most important aspect of Insurance, as if a Person is unhealthy due to his/her lack of discipline in lifestyle then it may arise many complications in future while if a Person is already having a disease before getting the Insurance, then it will definitely affect the sum Insured Corpus/Premium based upon the possibilities of life-threatening situations to take place due to the present disease.

- **Occupation & Income** – A Term life Insurance is meant to protect your family/dependents from financial crisis which means that they should not be indulged in the burden of lack of money at their difficult phase of losing the beloved ones.

  The Corpus needed to be insured should be at least 25 times the Annual Gross Salary of the Family Income.

  The Premium of a Term life Insurance is also decided by the kind of Occupation the person is employed, as if a person is involved into a life-threatening work then his/her Premium amount will be higher in comparison to the Person with a safe employment.

- **Place** – A Person living in a Place which is surrounded by different kinds of Pollution leading to unhealthy lifestyle causing negative effects on Physical as well as Psychological health will have a slight higher Premium as compared to a Person living in a peaceful locality with a clean environment along with access to all the amenities for healthcare and wellbeing.

## 2. Health Insurance –

The most important insurance, this is perhaps the most subscribed among all the Insurance types and is often misunderstood as the synonym of Insurance or to be the only insurance available in the market.

Today we are living in a world where we can't rely on our savings for the medical expenses that may suddenly arise and if you are not prepared then it may occur heavy on your pockets.

To conquer this problem of financing the medical expense of a Person and his/her family members, a Health insurance is required for an individual and family.

The factors associated with Life Insurance is also applicable to Health Insurance but the major focus is given on the Lifestyle & Diseases in which along with the Medical History of the person being Insured it is also taken into account if a Person is indulged in Smoking, Drinking Alcohol or any such harmful substance which will cause serious complications in future.

Types of Health Insurance –

I. <u>Individual Health Insurance</u> –
As the name suggests, it insures the healthcare medical assistance, checkup fees, and other sorts of medical expense for each member of a family. For example – If you have an individual health insurance for yourself, your spouse, your child, your mother and for your father a cover of ₹1000000 then each one of them can claim this amount individually per policy year against the insurance cover.

II. <u>Family Floater Health Insurance</u> –
It is similar to individual plan but the difference is that the sum insured will be shared with the family members in a policy year and each one of you won't be able to access it fully but partially in sharing. For example – If you have opted for a family floater plan for yourself and your spouse with a cover of ₹1000000 and if you exhausted the sum of ₹400000 then, your spouse will only be able to receive ₹600000 in a policy year.

III. <u>Senior Citizen Health Insurance</u> –
It is the most important sub-category of Health Insurance required for old age people who are most likely to get ill and need regular routine check-ups in the hospital. As it requires regular tests, it is slightly expensive in terms of premium paid to get the insurance cover.

IV. <u>Critical Illness Insurance</u> –
There are some diseases which have limited treatment options and the medications to it is very costly for a middle class individual to be able to afford it, such as Cancer, Heart stroke, Brain Stroke, Kidney Failure, etc. To overcome this problem, this Insurance cover is provided as an add-on to the primary health Insurance or can be availed separately as an individual plan.

V. <u>Maternity Insurance</u> –
It is a very important insurance needed for every newly married couple, as the process to plan a Baby and to have one is a long procedure with a lot of doctor's consultation, hospital visits for routine check-ups which can be very expensive on pockets and to avoid the financial stress it is opted as add-on policy.

## 3. **Vehicle Insurance** –

It is a mandatory Insurance which needs to be availed whenever a person buys or owns a Vehicle. It is required to insure that the third-party property if got damaged due to the insured vehicle can pay the loss to the property owner through the sum insured as per the terms and conditions mentioned in the policy.

There are two types of Insurance:

I. **Third-Party Insurance** –
It is the basic vehicle insurance mandatory for the vehicle owner to have which covers the loss or damage caused by the vehicle to the property got affected.

II. **Comprehensive Insurance** –
It is optional as per the rule but is highly recommended to have one because it not only provides cover against the damage to third-party property but also insures your damage cover to your insured vehicle.

There are several add-ons to it which are also very helpful to have in bad times!

# MUTUAL FUNDS

*"Investing is the Child of Savings which grows at a faster rate!"*

When I say the word 'Investment', what does it comes in your mind? Let me guess, may be Bank F.D/R.D, Gold, Land, etc. these are a few well known popular form of investments, but if we look at the R.O.I on these investments then, they beat inflation with very less margins. As a Bank F.D/R.D will fetch you around 6-8%, Gold will give around 8-10% and Land may provide 10-12% (depending upon the location of the area). Inflation is considered to be around 5-6%. So, if we calculate the margins offered by these investments then we see that, F.D/R.D gives +ve1-2%, Gold gives +ve3-4% whereas, Land gives around +ve5-6% and that means your Investments are barely growing when adjusted as per the inflation and it has also several deductions as per the taxation rules and additional making charges in case of Gold. I don't say it's bad, rather it is very good for conservative investors who are 60+yro but if it is done by the young investors who have a long time period to take the risk of volatility then, they need the exposure of Market Risks to generate a Corpus which is the multiple of the Amount Invested.

A short calculation was done in the earlier chapter (see page – 48-53), it was a short glimpse about Mutual Funds but now we will discuss about it elaborately.

Mutual Funds as the name suggests is a Fund which is made up of mutual contribution by the people and the amount accumulated also known as AUM (Asset under Management) are managed by a well qualified Fund Manager who works in an A.M.C (Asset Management Company).

It is mostly believed that the Mutual Funds only invest the money in Stock Market, but that's a Myth! Yes, Mutual Funds invest not only in Stock Market but also in Bond Markets, Mix of Both, in Foreign Markets and also in Commodity Markets as well.

So, let's explore them one by one and understand the right approach towards investment in these kinds of Mutual Funds.

Similar to Share price of a Stock in the Stock Market, Mutual Funds also has its own value which is known as N.A.V (Net Asset Value). When an A.M.C (Asset Management Company) launches a Fund then it is known as N.F.O (New Fund Offer) which provides a limited period offer of subscription when the N.A.V of the Fund is the lowest and as the period gets over then, the fluctuated N.A.V is reflected either increased/decreased as per the subscription quantity and Market scenarios (In most of the cases it is increased). EQUITY is said to be the Funds which invest majorly in Stock Market, whereas, DEBT is said to be the Funds which invests majorly in the Bond Market. While investing, you will see "Direct Plan" or "Regular Plan along with "Growth Plan" or "IDCW", Direct means that there's no intermediary commission involved in your investments whereas, Regular Plan is just opposite to it. In case of Growth, it means fund will compound your profits whereas, IDCW (Income Distribution Capital Withdrawal) will distribute your Profits!

## TYPES OF MUTUAL FUNDS:

There are two types of Mutual Funds –
    I.    CLOSED-ENDED FUNDS
    II.    OPEN-ENDED FUNDS

Generally Mutual Funds are considered to be an investment option as an alternative to direct stock market investing, it is an indirect way via Fund Manager but that's not the whole truth as discussed earlier but even those types were all the sub-category of Open-Ended Fund which is widely discussed whereas, the option of Closed-Ended Funds gets ignored by the investors but we will discuss about it as well!

I.    **CLOSED-ENDED FUNDS:-**
As the name suggests itself that the Fund type is closed in nature which means that it has a certain lock-in period until the Maturity, which simply means that once your Money got invested in it you will no more be able to get it back until it gets matured till the date of Maturity. Additionally, you will only be able to invest in it at the time of N.F.O, post the offer period you will not be able to invest.

The Closed-Ended Funds can be invested in the form of Equity Funds or Debt Funds. Although, majorly it is used as Debt Funds with Fixed Maturity Plans (also known as F.M.P) with maturity period ranging from few months to few years.

- Advantages –

    1. Fund Managers has full freedom over the Maturity period without having a burden of getting out of money due to frequent redemption requests as seen in the case of Open-Ended Funds where Investor withdraws money due to Market volatility and interrupts the Fund Manager's strategy to capture the investment opportunity in the volatile markets.

    2. Best for certain specific Goals which is to be planned in near future and can't be avoided, because of its specific maturity period and illiquid nature (money can't be withdrawn), most of the

A.M.Cs provide an indicative yield for Maturity (estimated R.O.I) which gives an idea of the maturity Amount.

3. As it is having a lock-in period till Maturity, it helps the investors to remain disciplined while investing and prevents them from timing the market (to transact as per the knowledge of investor without relying on the Fund Manager) for a Goal which is important for their Future.

- <u>Disadvantages</u> –

    1. Post Tax Returns are sometimes similar to that of Bank F.Ds which makes no sense to invest that too when illiquid nature of investment.

    2. Due to illiquid in nature, not suitable for investors who may require the money within the period of investment as it is not an investment alternative to your emergency funds.

3. The only method of Investment available in Closed-Ended Funds is by Lumpsum Investment (just like F.D).

Let's see how it works as per the Scenario of Investment –

A Person invests ₹100000 in an F.M.P with a Maturity Period of 1825 days (5years) and in the N.F.O; it shows an indicative yield of 9%.

Now, investments in mutual funds are calculated as XIRR (Extended Internal Rate of Return) which is applicable to S.I.P whereas, CAGR (Compounded Annual Growth Rate) is applicable to Lumpsum investment.

As F.M.P offers only Lumpsum, so we will calculate accordingly, $F.V = PV(1+r)^n$

Where,

F.V – Future Value (Maturity Amount)
P.V – Present Value (₹100000)
r – Rate of Interest (9%)
n – Number of Years (5 years)

$F.V = ₹100000(1+9\%)^5 =$ **₹153862** but let's consider fluctuations in the bond market which resulted to effective interest rate of

8% then, the Maturity Amount will be –
F.V = ₹100000(1+8%)$^5$ = **₹146933**

It shows that the Gross Maturity Amount will be 1.5x of the Principle Amount invested!

Before 2023, the investments made in Debt Funds was taxed according to the slab rates if sold before 3 years of time period whereas, if you hold for more than 3 years will charge 20% Tax with Indexation benefits (Taxed on Returns which are Inflation adjusted) but after 2023 Budget, now there will be taxation on Debt Funds according to your Income Tax slab rates regardless of the number of years you have been invested in it.

Let's take two scenarios,
SCENARIO – I: A person with 30% Income tax Slab will be taxed as,
Interest = F.V-P.V
=₹153862-₹100000=₹53862×30%=**₹16159**

SCENARIO – II: A person under 20% Income Tax Slab will be taxed as,
=₹153862-₹100000=₹53862×20%=**₹10772**

Difference = ₹16159-₹10772=**₹5387**!

II. **OPEN-ENDED FUND:-**

This is the most popular category of Mutual Funds, often misunderstood to be the only way to invest in Mutual Funds. As the name suggests that it is Open to invest across multiple sectors and allocations whereas, investors can easily withdraw their money which makes it a liquid investment.

There are several types of Open-Ended Funds which are categorized as follows –

1. **EQUITY** – The investments made in this is either majorly/purely invested into Stock Market through buying shares of the listed companies on Stock Exchange.

2. **DEBT** – When a Company wants to raise money by not selling their Shares but by providing Interest on the borrowed money as a Loan through Mutual Funds then, it is called as a Debt Fund.

3. <u>HYBRID</u> – As the name suggest, it is a mixed combination of both Equity and Debt Funds in different proportions as required.

4. <u>SOLUTION-ORIENTED</u> – Although it is not a very profound category but is offered by some AMCs and provides a focussed solution oriented approach to your investments designed to cater your specific Goals

5. <u>OTHERS</u> – Mostly ignored, yet a useful category which is offered by very few AMCs. It consists of some investments which cannot be categorized among any of the above mentioned categories due to its investment in different assets and markets.

Now, as we have a brief idea about different categories of funds, we can now understand them individually and analyze its advantages and disadvantages of investing in these asset classes through Mutual Funds.

# 1. EQUITY:

The word 'EQUITY' is very popular in the field of Business as it simply means the part of ownership of the Company by the Founder/Investor. Generally, it is said that when you buy a small portion of a stock listed on Stock Exchange then it is known as Shares, which when bought of a particular Company in percentage as per the valuation, then it is known as EQUITY.

As Mutual Funds invest in Bulk and buy a lot of Shares of a Company, it usually comes out to be a percentage ownership in the Company through Stock Exchange and thus it is known as Equity investing in Mutual Funds.

Before heading towards the details of sub-categorization, I would like to inform you that when you invest in Mutual Funds, then the expertise provided to you by the team of experts and Fund Manager is charged in the form of Expense Ratio which is a certain percentage (usually 0.5-3%) from your

R.O.I at the time of redemption. Whereas to prevent the rapid Money Fluctuations in the Fund, an 'Exit Load' is charged as a penalty for early redemption (usually they are of 1-2yrs). Although most of the A.M.Cs provide 'Active Mutual Fund' but 'Passive Mutual Fund' also plays a very important role in building a great portfolio for investing.

In Stock Market, there are few Indices (a group of similar stocks made to understand the Market Scenarios).
Ex. - Nifty50 Index, Sensex30 Index, Mid-Cap Index, etc, we will discuss about it in details in our next chapter.

In 'Passive Mutual Funds' the Fund Manager tries to replicate the allocation of an Index which produces similar returns on investment as given by an Index, due to its low research and Management of Funds they are cheaper in terms of Expense Ratio as compared with Active Mutual Funds.

Whereas, Active Mutual Funds are focussed on outperforming their Index by a margin which produces a higher return as compared to that from an Index. As they try to outperform the Index, they charge standard Expense Ratio which is higher as compared to that of Passive Mutual Funds.

Besides all of these, Mutual Fund investments are subject to Market Risk, please always read scheme related documents very carefully before investing.

1) **<u>Passive Mutual Funds</u>:**
There are many types of Passive Mutual Funds available in the Market and it is not possible to individually discuss each of them so we will cover the Funds which are widely available among A.M.Cs.

<u>Nifty Largecap Index Mutual Fund</u> –
'NIFTY' is the Index of NSE (National Stock Exchange) where the Top Companies with a sizable Market Share are listed and among them, the Top 100

Companies of India form the Nifty Largecap Index. As of June 2024, today the Market Size of Nifty50 is around ₹22,500 Crore.

Nifty Midcap Index Mutual Fund –
Similar to that of Nifty Largecap, Midcap Index has Top 101$^{st}$ to 250$^{th}$ Companies listed according to their decreasing order of Market share listed on NSE. As of June 2024, the Market Size of Nifty Midcap150 is around ₹20,000 Crore.

Nifty Smallcap Index Mutual Fund –
The most volatile Index among all the three, it has Top 251$^{st}$ and beyond Companies listed according to their decreasing order of Market share listed on NSE. As of June 2024, the Market Size of Nifty Smallcap250 is around ₹16,000 Crore.

There are many more Index present on NSE which are based upon some theme, commodity, etc. but these three are widely accepted and available among most of the A.M.Cs in the Market!

Now let's find out the ROI generated by investing in these three Index, we will calculate both S.I.P as well as Lumpsum investments.

**SCENARIO – I:** A Person invests ₹10,000/month as an S.I.P in Nifty50 Index Mutual Fund for 15 years.

In S.I.P it will be –

$F.V = P [(1+i)^n - 1] \times (1+i)/i$

Where,

F.V = Future Value
P = Amount you invest through S.I.P
i = Compounded rate of return
n = Investment duration in months
r = expected rate of return

Here, (r) = 14% (Past 15yrs performance from 2009-2024), (P) = ₹10000, (n) = 180, (i) = r/n = 14%/12 (12= months in a year) = 0.0116667.

$F.V = 10000\{[(1+0.0116666667)^{180} - 1]/0.0116666667 \times (1+0.0116666667)$
= **₹6128538**

Now, Lumpsum investment in Mutual Fund will be – $FV = PV(1+r)^n$

Where,

FV = Future value
PV = Present Value
r = rate of interest
n = number of years

Here, PV = ₹1800000, r = 14%, n = 15
So, ₹1800000 $(1+14\%)^{15}$ = **₹12848288**

As we can clearly see that the Maturity Amount in Lumpsum Investment is **2x** of the Maturity Amount calculated in S.I.P! This is simply because of the magic of Compounding which is entirely dependent on the Amount, Time invested and the Returns generated over that period of investment. But, do we have such a sizeable corpus with us to invest in the Markets? Most probably No, in that case even S.I.P isn't a bad option, but that been said don't be Sad as we are yet to discover the other two of them as well and also we will try to analyze the combination of these three Index.

**SCENARIO – II:** A Person invests ₹10000/month in Nifty Midcap150 Index Mutual Fund for 15 years.

In S.I.P it will be –

$F.V = P [(1+i)^n - 1] \times (1+i)/i$

Where,
F.V = Future Value
P = Amount you invest through S.I.P
i = Compounded rate of return
n = Investment duration in months
r = expected rate of return
Here, (r) = 20% (Past 15yrs performance from 2009-2024), (P) = ₹10000, (n) = 180, (i) = r/n = 20%/12 (12= months in a year) = 0.0166666667.

$F.V = 10000\{[(1+0.0166666667)^{180} - 1]/0.0166666667 \times (1+0.0166666667)$
= **₹11342949**

Now, Lumpsum investment in Mutual Fund will be – $FV = PV(1+r)^n$

Where,
FV = Future value
PV = Present Value
r = rate of interest
n = number of years

Here, PV = ₹1800000, r = 20%, n = 15
So, ₹1800000 (1+20%)$^{15}$ = **₹27732638**
Thus, the Maturity value of Lumpsum Investment is **2.44x** of the Investment in S.I.P!

**SCENARIO – III:** A Person invests 10000/month in Nifty Smallcap 250 Index Mutual Fund for 15 years.

In S.I.P it will be –

$$F.V = P [(1+i)^n - 1] \times (1+i)/i$$

Where,
F.V = Future Value
P = Amount you invest through S.I.P
i = Compounded rate of return
n = Investment duration in months
r = expected rate of return

Here, (r) = 17.6% (Past 15yrs performance from 2009-2024), (P) = ₹10000, (n) = 180, (i) = r/n = 17.6%/12 (12= months in a year) = 0.0146666667.

F.V=10000{[(1+0.0146666667)$^{180}$-1]/0.0146666667× (1+0.0146666667)
= **₹8818669**

Now, Lumpsum investment in Mutual Fund will be – FV = PV $(1+r)^n$

Where,

FV = Future value
PV = Present Value
r = rate of interest
n = number of years

Here, PV = ₹1800000, r = 17.6%, n = 15
So, ₹1800000 $(1+17.6\%)^{15}$ = **₹20482470**
Thus, the Maturity value of Lumpsum Investment is **2.32x** of the Investment in S.I.P!

Let's understand with the help of a Bar Chart –

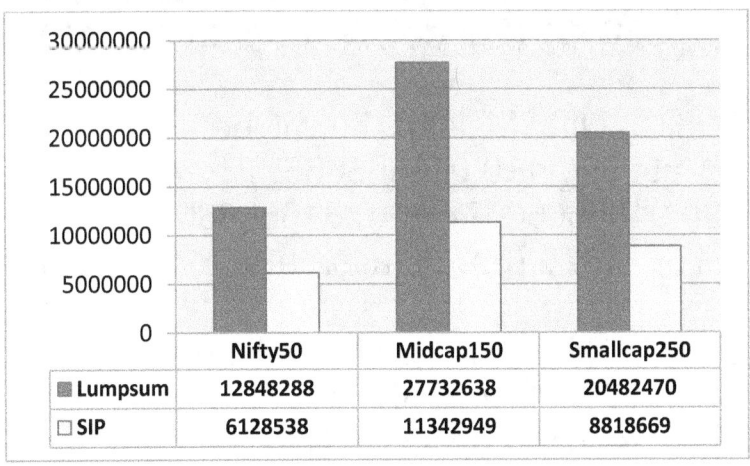

It is clearly visible that Midcap150 wins amongst them, but remember that Past returns are not Future predictions!!

In these Scenarios we were investing ₹10000/month separately to evaluate individual performance, but now we will try to mix and match among these Indices.

**In S.I.P –**

Let's take Nifty50 – 30%, Midcap150 – 50% and Smallcap250 – 20%

So, Nifty50 will have ₹3000, Midcap150 will have ₹5000 and Smallcap250 will have ₹2000 of Total ₹10000/month investment for 15yrs.

S.I.P in Nifty50 will be –
F.V=$3000\{[(1+0.0116666667)^{180}-1]/0.0116666667 \times (1+0.0116666667)$
= **₹1838561** (For details, refer to Pg-111)

S.I.P in Nifty Midcap150 will be –
F.V=$5000\{[(1+0.0166666667)^{180}-1]/0.0166666667 \times (1+0.0166666667)$
= **₹5671475** (For details, refer to Pg-113)

S.I.P in Nifty Smallcap250 will be –
F.V=$2000\{[(1+0.0146666667)^{180}-1]/0.0146666667 \times (1+0.0146666667)$
= **₹1763734** (For details, refer to Pg-114)

Thus, Total Maturity Corpus will be – **₹9273770!**

**In Lumpsum –**

Let's take Nifty50 – 30%, Midcap150 – 50% and Smallcap250 – 20%

So, Nifty50 will have ₹540000, Midcap150 will have ₹900000 and Smallcap250 will have ₹360000 of Total ₹1800000 Lumpsum investment.

Lumpsum in Nifty50 will be –
₹540000 $(1+14\%)^{15}$ = **₹3854487**
(For details, refer to Pg-112)

Lumpsum in Nifty Midcap150 will be –
₹900000 $(1+20\%)^{15}$ = **₹13866320**
(For details, refer to Pg-113-14)

Lumpsum in Nifty Smallcap250 will be –
₹360000 $(1+17.6\%)^{15}$ = **₹4096494**
(For details, refer to Pg-115)

Thus, Total Maturity Corpus will be –
**₹21817301**

Now if we compare S.I.P vs. Lumpsum then, Lumpsum is **2.35x** of S.I.P!

Similarly, you can yourself try various combinations and figure out what suits you the best. My suggestion would be to do a regular S.I.P and periodic Lumpsum investments whenever there's a Market Crash!!

## 2) **Active Mutual Funds:**

There are various kinds of Active Mutual Funds available in the Market and it is not possible to individually discuss each of them, so we will cover the Funds which are widely available among A.M.Cs. Active Mutual Funds can also be divided into 2 categories of Index Funds and Thematic Funds.

Although, Active Index Funds are more prevalent in Markets, it is suggested to consider Passive Index Funds over Active because most of the Fund Managers are unable to beat the Index with high margins due to which they are usually not able to outperform the benchmark index and upon that it has higher Exit Load and Expense Ratio for performing intense Research to beat the Index.

Thematic Funds on the other hand are the most Risky Funds to invest in a Mutual Fund because of its narrow investment portfolio and critical trades executed by Fund Managers.

As the name suggests, Thematic Mutual Funds are more concentrated upon the Theme of Sectors/Industries in which it primarily focuses rather than distributing the money among diverse companies based upon their Analysis of different Stocks.

Let's now discuss the commonly available Thematic Mutual Funds in the Market –

- <u>Energy Thematic Fund</u> –
  These kinds of Funds are focused on the Parameters of looking after the Companies evolving in the Energy sector theme, which has a potential to outperform its competitors in the Future or even better if it has a Monopoly in the Market.

- <u>Healthcare Thematic Fund</u> –
  Healthcare services and related fields are something which leads the Market because of it being a necessity and expensive to the pockets of Common Man. Fund Managers try to evaluate such companies which provides better services at minimal cost or is the

dominant player of its field, usually such companies have a very high market value but if it is fundamentally strong Company then, it is observed to buy it in the dip of a crash in the Market.

- <u>Technology Thematic Fund</u> –
  This is the Mother stream where innovation takes place to evolve other main stream Companies/Sectors in the Market. Technology based Companies helps different types of Core Industries to expand and work efficiently with the help of technological advancements in tools and accessories to minimize the Manual inputs and maximize the Automated Outputs.

- <u>Banking & Financial Thematic Fund</u> –
  These are the Funds which usually perform better as compared to any other Funds because of it being sector specific to Banking and Finance where the Fund Managers have the maximum expertise about the Markets because of being itself a part of the Industry.

Funds discussed further are taken as an example and is not an investment advice!

Now, let's explore the Returns on Investments done over a certain period of time through both S.I.P and Lumpsum Investments.

**SCENARIO – I:** A Person invests ₹10,000/month as an S.I.P in DSP Natural Resources and New Energy Mutual Fund for 11 years.

In S.I.P it will be –

F.V = P [(1+i) $^n$-1] × (1+i)/i

Where,

F.V = Future Value
P = Amount you invest through S.I.P
i = Compounded rate of return
n = Investment duration in months
r = expected rate of return

Here, (r) = 19.36% (Past 11yrs returns from Jan 2013-2024), (P) = ₹10000, (n) = 132, (i) = r/n = 19.36%/12 (12 = months in a year) = 0.0161333333.

F.V=10000{[(1+0.0161333333)$^{132}$-1]/0.01× (1+0.0161333333) = **₹4578738**

Now, Lumpsum investment in Mutual Fund will be – $FV = PV(1+r)^n$
Where,

FV = Future value
PV = Present Value
r = rate of interest
n = number of years

Here, PV = ₹1320000, r = 19.36%, n = 11
So, ₹1320000 $(1+19.36\%)^{11}$ = **₹9247426**
As expected, Lumpsum generates **2×** in comparison to S.I.P!

**SCENARIO – II:** A Person invests ₹10000/month in SBI Healthcare Opportunities Mutual Fund for 11 years.

In S.I.P it will be –

$F.V = P[(1+i)^n - 1] \times (1+i)/i$

Where,
F.V = Future Value
P = Amount you invest through S.I.P
i = Compounded rate of return
n = Investment duration in months
r = expected rate of return

Here, (r) = 19.26 %
(Past 11yrs performance from 20013-2024)

(P) = ₹10000, (n) = 132, (i) = r/n = 19.26%/12 (12= months in a year) = 0.01605.

$F.V = 10000\{[(1+0.01605)^{132}-1]/0.01605 \times (1+0.01605)\} = ₹4545765$

Now, Lumpsum investment in Mutual Fund will be – $FV = PV(1+r)^n$

Where,
FV = Future value
PV = Present Value
r = rate of interest
n = number of years

Here, PV = ₹1320000, r = 19.26%, n = 11
So, ₹1800000 $(1+19.26\%)^{15}$ = ₹9162559
Thus, the Maturity value of Lumpsum Investment is **2x** of the Investment in S.I.P!

**SCENARIO – III:** A Person invests ₹10,000/month as an S.I.P in ICICI Prudential Technology Mutual Fund for 11 years.

In S.I.P it will be –

$F.V = P[(1+i)^n - 1] \times (1+i)/i$

Where,

F.V = Future Value
P = Amount you invest through S.I.P
i = Compounded rate of return
n = Investment duration in months
r = expected rate of return

Here, (r) = 23.68% (Past 11yrs returns from Jan 2013-2024), (P) = ₹10000, (n) = 132, (i) = r/n = 23.68%/12 (12 = months in a year) = 0.0197333333.

$F.V = 10000\{[(1+0.0197333333)^{132}-1]/0.01 \times (1+0.0197333333)\}$ = **₹6299084**

Now, Lumpsum investment in Mutual Fund will be – $FV = PV(1+r)^n$
Where,

FV = Future value
PV = Present Value
r = rate of interest
n = number of years

Here, PV = ₹1320000, r = 23.68%, n = 11
So, ₹1320000 $(1+23.68\%)^{11}$ = **₹13673137**
As expected, Lumpsum generates **2.17×** in comparison to S.I.P!

**SCENARIO – IV:** A Person invests ₹10,000/month as an S.I.P in Nippon India Banking & Financial Services Mutual Fund for 11 years.

In S.I.P it will be –

$F.V = P [(1+i)^n - 1] \times (1+i)/i$

Where,

F.V = Future Value
P = Amount you invest through S.I.P
i = Compounded rate of return
n = Investment duration in months
r = expected rate of return

Here,
(r) = 15.22% (Past 11yrs returns from Jan 2013-2024)
(P) = ₹10000
(n) = 132
(i) = r/n = 15.22%/12 (12 = months in a year) = 0.0126833333.

$F.V = 10000\{[(1+0.0126833333)^{132} - 1]/0.01 \times (1+0.0126833333)\}$ = **₹3416235**

Now, Lumpsum investment in Mutual Fund will be – FV = PV $(1+r)^n$
Where,

FV = Future value
PV = Present Value
r = rate of interest
n = number of years

Here, PV = ₹1320000, r = 15.22%, n = 11
So, ₹1320000 $(1+15.22\%)^{11}$ = **₹6271631**

As expected, Lumpsum generates **1.83×** in comparison to S.I.P!

Let's now understand each scenario with the help of a Bar Chart –

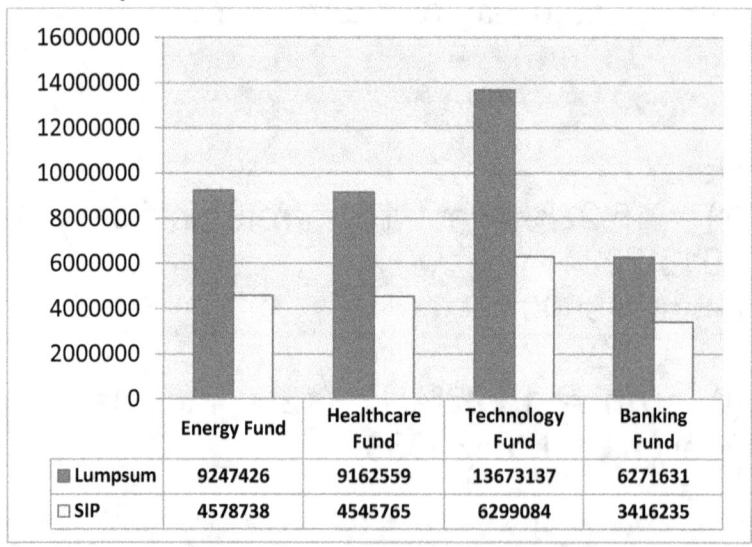

So, Technology Fund win's but remember that past returns are not assured in future!!

In these Scenarios we were investing ₹10000/month separately to evaluate individual performance, but now we will try to mix and match equally among these Indices.

**In S.I.P –**

Let's take Energy Fund – 25%, Healthcare Fund – 25%, Technology Fund – 25%, Banking Fund – 25%

So, Energy Fund will have ₹2500, Healthcare Fund will have ₹2500, Technology Fund will have ₹2500 and Banking Fund will have ₹2500 of Total ₹10000/month investment for 11yrs.

S.I.P in Energy Fund will be –

$F.V = 2500\{[(1+0.0161333333)^{132} - 1]/0.0161333333 \times (1+0.0161333333)$
= **₹1144685** (For details, refer to Pg-122)

S.I.P in Nifty Healthcare Fund will be –

$F.V = 2500\{[(1+0.01605)^{132} - 1]/0.01605 \times (1+0.01605)$ = **₹1136441** (For details, refer to Pg-123-24)

S.I.P in Technology Fund will be –

F.V=2500{[(1+0.0197333333)$^{132}$-1]/0.01× (1+0.0197333333) = ₹**1574771**
(For details, refer to Pg-124-125)

S.I.P in Banking Fund will be –

F.V=2500{[(1+0.0126833333)$^{132}$-1]/0.01× (1+0.0126833333) = ₹**854059**

Thus, Total Maturity Corpus will be – **₹4709956!**

**In Lumpsum –**
Let's take Energy Fund – 25%, Healthcare Fund – 25%, Technology Fund – 25%, Banking Fund – 25%
So, Energy Fund will have ₹330000, Healthcare Fund will have ₹330000, Technology Fund will have ₹330000 and Banking Fund will have ₹330000 of Total ₹1320000 investment for 11yrs.

Lumpsum in Energy Fund will be –

₹330000 (1+19.36%) $^{11}$ = ₹**2311856**
(For details, refer to Pg-123)

Lumpsum in Healthcare Fund will be –

₹330000 $(1+19.26\%)^{11}$ = **₹2290640**
(For details, refer to Pg-124)

Lumpsum in Technology Fund will be –

₹330000 $(1+23.68\%)^{11}$ = **₹3418284**
(For details, refer to Pg-125)

Lumpsum for Banking Fund will be –

₹330000 $(1+15.22\%)^{11}$ = **₹1567908**
(For details, refer to Pg-127)

Thus, Total Maturity Corpus will be –
**₹9588688**

Now if we compare S.I.P vs. Lumpsum then, Lumpsum is **2x** of S.I.P!

Similarly, you can yourself try various combinations and figure out what suits you the best. My suggestion would be to do a regular S.I.P and periodic Lumpsum investments whenever there's a Market Crash (When Market Index falls more than 10%)!!

## 2. DEBT FUNDS:

These Funds are not so popular investments due to its low volatility and stable returns but are very essential in one's portfolio as it diversifies your investments apart from Equity, which provides stability when there is a Market Correction.

'Debt' word simply means Loan, which investors lend to Companies as well as Govt. against which the Borrower provides a fixed rate of return which gets influenced by certain factors like Interest rate cycle, Credit rating of the Companies, etc.

The Companies in which the Fund Managers lend investor's money through Debt Securities (medium of lending agreement which provides information about Maturity date, Interest rate, etc.) are classified in 4 categories as per its Credit rating decided by Credit Rating Agency (CRA) –

1) **AAA** – Securities with this rating have the highest degree of Safety against any Financial Obligation. Thus, the Credit Risk is the lowest in it.

2) **AA** – These Securities have the second highest degree of Safety and thus, have very low Credit Risk

3) **A** – Securities with this rating are considered to have adequate degree of Safety and thus, have relatively low Credit Risk.

4) **BBB** – Securities with this rating are considered to have moderate level of Safety and thus, have moderate Credit Risk.

5) **BB** – These Securities have moderate risk of defaulting debt and getting indulged in any Financial Obligations.

6) **B** – These Securities have high Risk of defaulting and getting indulged in any Financial Obligations.

7) **C** – These Securities have very high Risk of defaulting and getting indulged in any Financial Obligations.

8) **D** – These Securities are either in Default or may get into near Future.

Amongst all the Securities mentioned based upon its Credit Risk rating, Fund Managers have to choose a right balance for their investment requirements as because it is generally seen that the Securities with high risk tend to provide high returns on debt, but everything comes at a cost and here it is the risk of getting default whereas, if opted for AAA category then no doubt the returns are somewhat guaranteed but will not provide better returns even if compared to an FD. So, the right approach according to the investment duration, objective needs to be taken into consideration while investing in these Securities by the Mutual Fund Managers.

Accordingly, there are several categories of Debt Mutual Funds such as –

- <u>Long Duration Funds</u> –
  These are the Funds which invest in Bonds issued by Government/Private entities for duration more than 5-7yrs of Maturity period. This Fund is ideal for accumulating a Corpus which is needed in between 5-10yrs but are flexible in terms of the monetary requirement for the purpose to be achieved through this Investment.

- <u>Medium Duration Funds</u> –
  These are very similar to that of long duration funds but comes with a lesser maturity period of government/private bonds generally of 3-5yrs of time period, so the ideal duration of investment would be 5-7yrs of time horizon with flexibility on the amount of returns generated in that Fund.

- <u>Short Duration Fund</u> –
  As having shorter maturity period, the Fund would generate comparatively lower returns if compared to long or medium duration funds because the Fund Manager would focus more on securities which are AAA/AA category so that the debt doesn't gets defaulted due to shorter duration of maturity period, it is generally of 1-2yrs of time horizon.

- <u>Gilt Funds</u> –
  These are the Funds which purely invests in Government securities of 5yrs or 10yrs Maturity period and as they are backed by the Government bodies, thus the returns are somewhat guaranteed with fluctuations due to transaction in those funds or interest rate cycles.

- <u>Dynamic Bond Fund</u> –
  These are the Funds which are not bounded to the investment durations due to maturity period of the bonds rather here; the Fund Manager has full freedom to invest among securities with varying maturity period of investments so that the investors can get an average of all securities with different duration of maturity.

  There are several other types of Debt Funds but these are the widely used and available categories amongst all of them.

3. **<u>HYBRID</u>:**

   As the name suggests, it is a mix of different asset classes of investment, it is a very important category because of the inherit diversification of funds done by the Fund Managers as per the Market's requirements and sentiments towards the volatility of the asset class performing in the Open Markets. Often, this category is misunderstood as the only mix of Equity and Debt Funds but that's not true. Yes, there are also other asset classes discussed further.

- Equity Oriented Hybrid Funds –
  This is the Fund which is generally suggested by the advisors for the first time investors entering into the world of Investing in Mutual Funds. As the name suggests, it needs to have a higher proportion of ≥65% in Equity whereas, ≤35% in Debt instruments to create a perfect balance by the Fund Manager according to the Market scenarios.

- Debt-Oriented Hybrid Funds –
  Mostly ignored by the Investors because of its limitations in providing high returns due to large allocation in Debt Funds(≥60%), this Fund is meant for the people who want stable returns on their investment which is comparatively higher than the FDs and Bonds due to its small investments in Equity(≤40%).

- Balanced Funds –
  It is a Fund which is advised to be a part of your investment even in a small portion because as the name suggests, it balances itself according to the Market scenarios within Debt-Equity or other investment categories. Hence, provides lucrative returns on investments.

Debt Funds/Debt Hybrid Funds are made in such a way that it could provide stable returns to tackle the volatility of the Equity while generating better returns than any of the traditional investments. It is generally advised that as you are getting close to your retirement, you should gradually increase the allocation of Debt Hybrid Funds and after retirement the maximum corpus should be invested in the Debt Funds.

Let's do a Comparative ROI Analysis of different types of Debt Funds as well as Hybrid Funds:

### SCENARIO – I:

A Person invests ₹500000 Lumpsum in ICICI Prudential Long Term Bond Fund for 10 years of investment period.

Lumpsum investment in Mutual Fund will be – $FV = PV(1+r)^n$

Where,

FV = Future value
PV = Present Value
r = rate of interest
n = number of years

Here, PV = ₹500000, r = 8.15%, n = 10
So, $₹500000 (1+8.15\%)^{10}$ = **₹1094549**

## SCENARIO – II:

A Person invests ₹500000 Lumpsum in Aditya Birla Sun Life Medium Term Plan for 5 years of investment period.

Lumpsum investment in Mutual Fund will be – $FV = PV(1+r)^n$

Where,
FV = Future value
PV = Present Value
r = rate of interest
n = number of years

Here, PV = ₹500000, r = 12%, n = 5
So, $₹500000(1+12\%)^5$ = **₹881171**

## SCENARIO – III:

A Person invests ₹500000 Lumpsum in ICICI Prudential Short Term Fund for 3 years of investment period.

Lumpsum investment in Mutual Fund will be – $FV = PV(1+r)^n$

Where,
FV = Future value
PV = Present Value
r = rate of interest
n = number of years

Here, PV = ₹500000, r = 7.18%, n = 3
So, $₹500000(1+7.18\%)^3$ = **₹615618**

## SCENARIO – IV:

A Person invests ₹500000 Lumpsum in Nippon India Gilt Securities Fund for 10 years of investment period.

Lumpsum investment in Mutual Fund will be – $FV = PV(1+r)^n$

Where,
FV = Future value
PV = Present Value
r = rate of interest
n = number of years

Here, PV = ₹500000, r = 8.98%, n = 10
So, ₹500000 $(1+8.98\%)^{10}$ = **₹1181512**

## SCENARIO – V:

A Person invests ₹500000 Lumpsum in UTI Dynamic Bond Fund for 5 years of investment period.

Lumpsum investment in Mutual Fund will be – $FV = PV(1+r)^n$

Where,
FV = Future value
PV = Present Value
r = rate of interest
n = number of years

Here, PV = ₹500000, r = 8.91%, n = 5
So, ₹500000 $(1+8.91\%)^5$ = **₹766141**

Now, if we do the comparison through a Bar Chart Analysis then we see that –

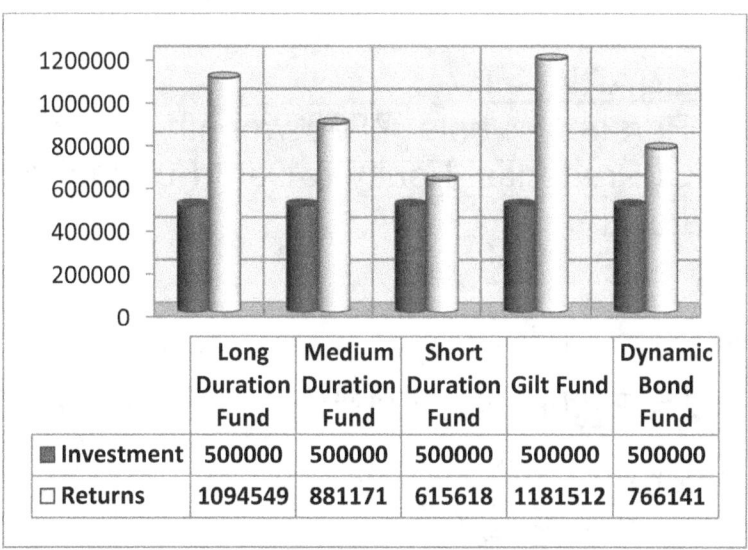

|  | Long Duration Fund | Medium Duration Fund | Short Duration Fund | Gilt Fund | Dynamic Bond Fund |
|---|---|---|---|---|---|
| Investment | 500000 | 500000 | 500000 | 500000 | 500000 |
| Returns | 1094549 | 881171 | 615618 | 1181512 | 766141 |

No doubt Gilt Funds became the winner but, it is important to understand that the Returns generated in these funds are not guaranteed in future and neither are they supposed to deliver returns matching Equity because Debt is by design made to generate stable returns focusing more on the Capital Protection.

We didn't calculated S.I.P because Debt Funds are meant to be invested when you are about to withdrawal after sometime and thus switching your existing Investments in Equity into Debt or new Lumpsum investment is more worth it.

Now let's evaluate the Returns generated by the Hybrid Funds –

### **SCENARIO – I:**
A Person invests ₹5000/month S.I.P in ICICI Prudential Equity & Debt Fund for 10 years.

In S.I.P it will be –

$$F.V = P [(1+i)^n - 1] \times (1+i)/i$$

Where,
F.V = Future Value
P = Amount you invest through S.I.P
i = Compounded rate of return
n = Investment duration in months
r = expected rate of return

Here, (r) = 16.18% (Past 10yrs performance), (P) = ₹5000, (n) = 120, (i) = r/n = 16.18%/12 (12 = months in a year) = 0.0134833333.

$$F.V = 5000\{[(1+0.0134833333)^{120} - 1]/0.0134833333 \times (1+0.0134833333)\}$$
= **₹1499092**

## SCENARIO – II:

A Person invests ₹5000/month S.I.P in Kotak Debt Hybrid Fund for 10 years.

In S.I.P it will be –

$$F.V = P[(1+i)^n - 1] \times (1+i)/i$$

Where,
F.V = Future Value
P = Amount you invest through S.I.P
i = Compounded rate of return
n = Investment duration in months
r = expected rate of return

Here,
(r) = 10.98% (Past 5yrs performance),
(P) = ₹5000, (n) = 120,
(i) = r/n = 10.98%/12 (12= months in a year) = 0.00915

$$F.V = 5000\{[(1+0.00915)^{120} - 1]/0.00915 \times (1+0.00915)\} = ₹1093649$$

## SCENARIO – III:

A Person invests ₹5000/month S.I.P in ICICI Prudential Multi-Asset Fund for 10 years.

In S.I.P it will be –

$$F.V = P [(1+i)^n - 1] \times (1+i)/i$$

Where,
F.V = Future Value
P = Amount you invest through S.I.P
i = Compounded rate of return
n = Investment duration in months
r = expected rate of return

Here,
(r) = 14.85% (Past 10yrs performance),
(P) = ₹5000, (n) = 120,
(i) = r/n = 14.85%/12 (12= months in a year) = 0.012375

$$F.V = 5000\{[(1+0.012375)^{120} - 1]/0.012375 \times (1+0.012375)\} = ₹1380476$$

Now, if we do the comparison through a Bar Chart Analysis then we see that –

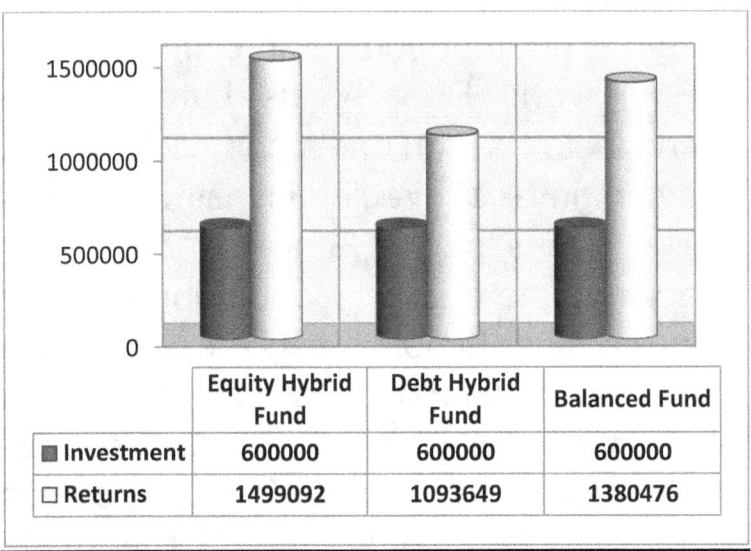

| | Equity Hybrid Fund | Debt Hybrid Fund | Balanced Fund |
|---|---|---|---|
| Investment | 600000 | 600000 | 600000 |
| Returns | 1499092 | 1093649 | 1380476 |

No doubt Equity Hybrid Funds became the winner but, it is important to understand that the Returns generated in these funds are not guaranteed in future.

It is important to understand that due to high exposure of Equity, the Equity Hybrid Fund outperformed other two funds but everything comes at a price. Thus, even though Equity Hybrid Fund produced better returns but is also volatile and may also affect the invested corpus substantially during the period of investment.

## 4. SOLUTION ORIENTED FUND:

These Funds are provided by few AMCs as it is not that popular in comparison to Equity and Debt Funds but are very crucial to have in one's portfolio to attain a certain Goal directed investment.

The Focus of the Fund Manager is to achieve the desired Goal of the investor in the given timelines and accordingly it invests in different Asset classes which suit the best considering the Financial Markets. In most of the Funds, it comes with a lock-in period (investments made will be locked in for that period) it is done to ensure that the Corpus stays invested to overcome the disturbance in compounding and impulsive withdraws of funds for Liquidity.

Generally, these are of two types:

- Retirement – Oriented Funds –
  As it is clear by the name itself that the Fund is purely focused on Retirement Planning of the Investor and thus, will be investing in desired asset as per the market scenarios, targeted corpus, time allotted for investment.

- <u>Children Benefit Fund</u> –
  Similar to the previously discussed fund, it is also focused on the desired goal of investment which is generally Marriage of the Child or to have enough corpuses for the Child's higher education.

Let's understand each of them with the help of different scenarios:

## **SCENARIO – I:**
A 30yro Person invests ₹15000/month S.I.P in ICICI Prudential Retirement Fund for 30 years.

The scheme has two options of Auto/Active Choice of investment divided into 4 sub categories of investment fund type as –

<u>Pure Equity Plan</u> –

This Plan offers maximum investment in Equity and is considered suitable for people in the age group of 25-45 years.

<u>Hybrid Aggressive Plan</u> –

It acts as an Equity Hybrid Fund and it allows some investment of Debt and is considered suitable for people in the age group of 46-50 years.

## Hybrid Comprehensive Plan –

It acts as a Debt Hybrid Fund and has a maximum investment in Debt along with some allocation to Equity and is considered suitable for people in the age group of 51-56 years.

## Pure Debt Plan –

This plan allows maximum investment in Debt and is considered suitable for people in the age group of 56-60 years

It also comes with a lock-in period of 5 years (cannot withdraw the invested corpus during this time period).

If Chosen for Auto Investment plan then it will automatically invest the corpus according to the age of the investor to reach the desired retirement corpus at the age of 60.

The particular fund has outperformed its competitors in the last 5 years of investment horizon so it has been taken for calculation, but its present returns can't guarantee future returns and thus, it is not a recommendation. It has been used as an example to understand the unique solution oriented methodology of investment provided by this Fund.

So, we will need to calculate the returns individually in every Asset Allocation Fund as Auto choice investment according to age.

## Pure Equity Plan –

In S.I.P it will be –

$$F.V = P [(1+i)^n - 1] \times (1+i)/i$$

Where,
F.V = Future Value
P = Amount you invest through S.I.P
i = Compounded rate of return
n = Investment duration in months
r = expected rate of return

Here,
(r) = 15% (assuming on pure Equity),
(P) = ₹15000,
(n) = 180 (15yrs – 30yro-45yro),
(i) = r/n = 15%/12 (12 = months in a year)
= 0.0125

$$F.V = 15000\{[(1+0.0125)^{180} - 1]/0.0125 \times (1+0.0125)\} = ₹10152946$$

Now after the age crosses 45, then it will be automatically reinvested in Hybrid Aggressive Plan.

So, let's take Lumpsum investment of ₹10152946 for 5 years and continue our SIP of ₹15000 till the age of 50.

Lumpsum investment in Mutual Fund will be – FV = PV $(1+r)^n$

Where,
FV = Future value
PV = Present Value
r = rate of interest
n = number of years

Here,
PV = ₹10152946,
r = 12% (assuming in equity hybrid),
n = 5

So, ₹10152946 $(1+12\%)^5$ = **₹17892960**

Whereas, In case of SIP (assuming 12%) –

F.V=15000$\{[(1+0.01)^{60}-1]/0.01 \times (1+0.01)$ = **₹1237295**

Thus, Total –

₹17892960+₹1237295 = **₹19130255**

Now after the age crosses 50, then it will be automatically reinvested in Hybrid Comprehensive Plan.

So, let's take Lumpsum investment of ₹19130255 for 5 years and continue our SIP of ₹15000 till the age of 55.

Lumpsum investment in Mutual Fund will be – $FV = PV(1+r)^n$

Where,
FV = Future value
PV = Present Value
r = rate of interest
n = number of years

Here,
PV = ₹19130255,
r = 10% (assuming in debt hybrid),
n = 5

So, ₹19130255 $(1+10\%)^5$ = **₹30809467**

Whereas, In case of SIP (assuming 10%) –

$F.V = 15000\{[(1+0.0083333333)^{60} - 1]/0.0083333333 \times (1+0.0083333333)$ = **₹1171236**

Thus, Total – ₹30809467 + ₹1171236 = **₹31980703**

Now after the age crosses 55, then it will be automatically reinvested in Hybrid Comprehensive Plan.

So, let's take Lumpsum investment of ₹31980703 for 5 years and continue our SIP of ₹15000 till the age of 60.

Lumpsum investment in Mutual Fund will be – $FV = PV(1+r)^n$

Where,
FV = Future value
PV = Present Value
r = rate of interest
n = number of years

Here,
PV = ₹31980703,
r = 8% (assuming in debt),
n = 5

So, ₹31980703 $(1+8\%)^5$ = **₹46990145**

Whereas, In case of SIP (assuming 8%) –

$F.V = 15000\{[(1+0.0066666667)^{60} - 1]/0.0066666667 \times (1+0.0066666667)$ = **₹1109500**

Thus, Total – ₹46990145+₹1109500 = **₹48099645**

Hence at the age of 60, the person will be having around ₹4.81Crore.

In the world of Finance, it is said that ideally 50% of your Income should be your monthly expense, 20% on entertainment whereas, 30% should be invested.

Assuming the Person investing ₹15000 per month was investing 30% of his monthly salary means that his monthly income will be ₹50000 per month.

Now if we assume 6% inflation every year then, in the next 30 years, the Inflation adjusted amount will be –

$FV = PV (1+r)^n$

Where,
FV = Future value
PV = Present Value
r = rate of interest
n = number of years

$FV = ₹50000 (1+6\%)^{30}$ = **₹287174**
So, at the age of 60 you will need ₹287174 per month to sustain your present income. But if you observed, monthly expense and desire was combined 70% (50% on needs + 20% on desire) of the monthly income.

Thus, you technically need 70% of ₹50000 i.e. ₹35000 per month inflation adjusted after 30 years to live your life after retirement.

So, FV = ₹35000 $(1+6\%)^{30}$ = **₹201022**

Now, let us assume that you put the Maturity Corpus in a Fixed Deposit of a Bank which provides 7.10%p.a for 10 year time period.

Then, if we do an FD of ₹34000000 at 7.10%p.a for 10 years will provide us ₹2414000p.a or **₹201167/month** after setting it for monthly payout of interest.

Whereas, the remaining Amount ₹48099645-34000000 = **₹14099645** can be put in a cumulative FD in several parts ensuring any Emergency on Medical ground or Marriage of Kids, etc.

Please note –

The Calculations shown above is just for illustrative purpose and does not guarantee this kind of return provided by any bank and neither has it taken account of any Tax applicable to the Capital gains on investments made, as it may vary from fund to fund. Thus, investors are suggested to be informed before investing in any Mutual Fund.

## SCENARIO – II:

A Person invests ₹15000/month SIP in HDFC Children's Gift Fund for 10 years.

The Scheme comes with a lock-in period of 5 years to ensure the corpus remains protected from impulsive withdraws.

In S.I.P it will be –

$$F.V = P [(1+i)^n - 1] \times (1+i)/i$$

Where,
F.V = Future Value
P = Amount you invest through S.I.P
i = Compounded rate of return
n = Investment duration in months
r = expected rate of return

Here,
(r) = 17.29% (historical returns for 10yrs),
(P) = ₹15000,
(n) = 120 (10yrs),
(i) = r/n = 17.29%/12 (12 = months in a year) = 0.0144083333

$$F.V = 15000\{[(1+0.0144083333)^{120} - 1]/0.0144083333 \times (1+0.0144083333) = ₹4821905$$

Thus after 10 years of investment, the person will have ₹4821905 (post Tax, the amount will be less as per the Tax policy applicable in that Financial Year) which he/she could use for his/her child's education and future ambitions.

## 5. **OTHER FUNDS:**

These are the Funds which cannot be classified in any other category and thus are placed as miscellaneous Funds, it is generally seen that investors are mostly unaware of these Funds. But, these Funds are also important to have in one's portfolio as it provides a nice diversification among all other category of investments.

Mainly, these are of three types –

- ETF Fund –
  Exchange Traded Fund (ETF) is unique from other Funds as it is traded on Stock Market as shares and you need to have a Demat Account to execute transactions in these Funds. They usually represent a theme, sector, index and allows you to invest in the entire basket with a very minimum amount as low as ₹100 which further gets split as

per the proportion of the investment category.

For Example – Nifty100 ETF will invest your money in equal proportion as the companies are listed on the Stock Exchange.

- <u>FOF</u> –

    Fund of Funds (FOF) are those Funds which are available for investors to invest in either multiple mutual funds in a single investment or allows you to invest in an instrument which is not directly available through Mutual Fund or they invest in a Foreign Mutual Fund/Stocks which might not be easily accessible to the investors.

- <u>Commodity Fund</u> –

    These are the Funds which either invests in Gold or Silver in the form of ETF through Exchange or buying Funds which invests in ETF as investing indirectly in the form of Fund of Funds.

Now, as we have understood each of them, let's observe through examples in the form of different Scenarios.

## SCENARIO – I:

A Person buys 3846 units of Nippon India ETF Nifty 50 BeES at ₹130 on Dec 2019 and holds it for 5years, he sell his units on Dec 2024 at ₹274 on the Stock Exchange.

So, ₹130×3846 = ₹499980 (invested)

After 5 years, ₹274×3846 = ₹1053804 (credited in Demat Account)

Thus, Profit made will be –

₹1053804 - ₹499980 = ₹553824

## SCENARIO – II:

A Person invests ₹500000 Lumpsum in ICICI Prudential US Bluechip Equity Direct Fund for 10 years.

Lumpsum investment in Mutual Fund will be – $FV = PV(1+r)^n$

Where,
FV = Future value
PV = Present Value
r = rate of interest
n = number of years

Here,
PV = ₹500000,
r = 17% (10yrs historical returns),
n = 10

So, ₹500000 $(1+17\%)^{10}$ = **₹2403414**

## SCENARIO – III:
A Person invests ₹500000 Lumpsum in SBI Gold Fund for 5 years.

Lumpsum investment in Mutual Fund will be – FV = PV $(1+r)^n$

Where,
FV = Future value
PV = Present Value
r = rate of interest
n = number of years

Here,
PV = ₹500000,
r = 14.3% (5yrs historical returns),
n = 5

So, ₹500000 $(1+14.3\%)^5$ = **₹975441**

*That's all for Mutual Funds, always remember that high Returns comes at a cost of high Risk. Invest Smartly!*

# Introducing Stock Market
*"The Only way an Employee can become Owner is becoming a Shareholder!"*

The above written statement may appear to be silly, but that's the truth. If you are working in a Company which is listed on the Stock Market and you have a strong belief on the Management and Future of the Company, then buying Shares would not only give you good returns but will over the years of continuous accumulation of Shares can lead to you becoming a Shark Investor in the Company which will allow you to be the part of the Top Management and Board Member.

Now you may feel it to be extremely Risky and have heard about People losing all their hard-earned money in this deep well of Stock Market. Well, even that is also true for most of the People who 'Gamble' in the name of 'Investing'. If you treat it as a lottery to make Overnight 100x Money, then surely you would end up with empty hands.

Always remember that Stock Market is an Exchange, where the Shares of the listed Company are traded among Sellers and Buyers. Whereas, price movement/volatility depends upon lot of factors which may be directly or even indirectly influence the Market sentiments.

In short if you know how it works, then it will be your Best Investment whereas, if you follow someone blindly will lead to a Financial Crisis in Future.

Let's now understand each and every Terminology/Jargons –

- **Exchange** – It is a Marketplace where the Stocks are transacted in the form of Shares. Ex. – BSE, NSE
- **IPO** – Initial Public Offering (IPO) is said when a Company lists its Stock for the first time in the Market; Investors are allowed to invest in 'Lot Size'.
- **Stock** – When a Company is listed on the Stock Exchange, then it is called as a Stock.
- **Share** – The Equity distribution done in small quantities of the Stock in the Market is said as a Share.
- **Demat Account** – De-Materialized Account is where the transactions of Shares take place in the Stock Exchange.
- **Broker** – It is the Agent which acts as a mediator in between the Investors or Traders and the Exchange helping to

execute the Transactions seamlessly without any hassle.
- **Brokerage** – It is the charge taken by the Brokers to avail the Service for better execution of Transactions and bear the cost of availing the service.
- **Bull Market (Bullish)** – When the Market continuously moves in upward direction then, it is known as a Bull Market.
- **Bear Market (Bearish)** – When the Market continuously moves in the downward direction then, it is known as a Bear Market.
- **Trend** – It is a term used to understand the general Market movement, it can be a Bearish Trend, Bullish Trend or Sideways Trend.
- **Dividend** – When the Company distributes its profits in the form of additional shares in a fraction to the Shareholder is known as Dividend.
- **Stock Split** – When the Company listed on the Exchange decides to Split the Stock Valuation in a ratio to decrease the Stock price and increase the number of Shares is known as a Stock Split. It does not affect the valuation but adds multiple Shares in the Market making the Stock more accessible.

- **Bonus Share** – When a Company announces to give additional shares to the Shareholder as a Gift/Bonus is known as Bonus Share. It is decided in the form of a ratio and it significantly affects the Stock price in the Market.
- **Face Value** – It is the nominal value of the Share which is used in calculating corporate actions as Dividends, Splits, Bonus, etc.
- **52 Week high/low** – It is a term used to indicate that the particular Stock price is at its lowest/highest in a Year/52 Weeks
- **Upper/Lower Circuit** – It is a term used to indicate that the Stock has been at its highest/lowest price in a Trading day.
- **Position** – When a person buy/sell Shares of a Stock then, it is traded in the Exchange till the Market closes which after that gets clear if it is a Profit/Loss. The time frame after buying/selling till the Market closes is known as Position.
- **Square-Off** – After holding the Position, when the Market closes then the transaction executed in the Demat Account is known as Square-Off.
- **Volume** – The number of transactions executed in the Stock in a trading session is known as Volume.

There are many more Terminologies yet to be discovered but we shall only focus on those which are important for us.

So, there are mainly two types of People in the Market –

**TRADERS** – The Person who tries to book Profits in a short period of time by trading in the Market are known as Traders.

**INVESTORS** – The Person who holds the Shares of a particular Stock for Long Term Capital gains are known as Investors.

In this Chapter, we will be focusing more on the Investing part and will learn basics on Trading.

There are mainly two types of Trading Practices commonly used –

- **Intra-Day Trading** – When a Trader tries to gain Profits in a Single Day (9:00 A.M to 3:30P.M) is known as Intraday Trading.
- **Swing Trading** – When a Trader tries to gain Profits following a 'Trend' pattern in several days to maximum one month is known as Swing Trading.

The Technique used is known as Technical Analysis, to be discussed later.

Apart from these two, there is also a category which is very lucrative because of the Returns it delivers but is 'The Most Risky' among anything in Stock Market. These are the 'Derivatives'.

**DERIVATIVES** – It is an Instrument or Contract which derives its own value from an Underlying Asset.

Example –

Let's suppose you have a Locker worth ₹10000 and in that Locker you have kept ₹100000 Cash, now what is the value of your Locker, is it still ₹10000? NO, as it also has ₹100000 Cash in it which combined makes it worth ₹10000+₹100000 = ₹110000. Thus, the value of the Locker is being derived by its Underlying Asset which in this case is ₹100000 Cash!

They are of 4 Types –

- **FORWARD** – It is a Contract between a Buyer and a Seller to settle on a fixed Price rate of the Commodity in advance to avoid unfavorable Price fluctuations in Future.
  Example –
  A Person wants to buy a Gold Jewellery for wearing in the Festive season but is

aware that the Price of Gold will rise in the Festivals due to high demand and wants to buy it now, but doesn't has the required Amount because the Final Cost of the Jewellery will include –
Gold Rate + Making Charges + GST

So, he signs a Forward Contract that he will lock the Price of Gold by paying some Money in advance and will pay the rest amount in Future irrespective of the Price fluctuations.
Now if the Price of Gold rises then the Person will be in Profit, whereas if the Price decreases then he will be in Loss. Thus, it is a Zero-Sum Deal!

- **FUTURES** – It is same as 'Forward' with a Regulating Authority which ensures that the Deal takes place without violating agreement by either of the participants.
  In case of the Stock Market, it is SEBI (Securities Exchange Board of India) which takes care of the transparency in each and every transaction or Contract being made in Futures/Options.
  Futures contract of Stocks, Commodity, Currency and Index are easily available and traded on Stock Exchange.

Let us understand Futures with a simple Example –

There is a Stock-A of ₹5000/Share and you know that the Price of this Share will reach ₹7000/Share after 2 months and you want to buy the Stock. There are two ways of Buying it, firstly you can Buy 1 share and wait for 2 months and if the Share rises up to ₹7000 then you gain a Profit of ₹2000 but, Secondly your Stock Broker provides you a Future Contract of the Stock-A with Leverage (extra money as a Loan) which is usually 80-90% of the Share Price.

That means, you can buy a Future Contract of Stock-A at the price of ₹500-1000/Share (10-20% of the Actual price, as remaining 80-90% provided as Leverage by the Stock Broker).

It is to be noted that Future Contract of the Share is always provided in Lot-size (varies in different stocks but usually lies in the range of 100-300).

Also it has three different dates of Expiry (Date on which the Futures Contract will be executed as per the Market Conditions) which are – Near Month (after 1 month), Next Month (after 2 month) and Far Month (after 3 month).

Now, let's suppose that Future Contract of Stock-A is present on the Stock Exchange on three Expiry dates of 12$^{th}$ March, 12$^{th}$ April and 12$^{th}$ May as of present date say, 12$^{th}$ Feb.

So, you will have these three options available on the Stock Exchange –

Stock-A FUT 12 Mar 25 (Near Month)
Stock-A FUT 12 Apr 25 (Next Month)
Stock-A FUT 12 May 25 (Far Month)

Let's Analyze according to different scenarios –

**<u>SCENARIO – I:</u>**
Stock-A is valued at ₹5000/Share on 12$^{th}$ Feb and you Buy 1 Lot (200 shares) of Stock-A FUT 12 Apr 25 at 700/Share (Leverage of 86% of the Corpus on interest of 3% per month).

So, 1 Lot = 200 Shares at ₹700 = ₹140000
And if it hits ₹7000/Share then, you will get (₹7000-₹5000) × 200 = ₹400000
As, you just booked the Lot on a Margin of 14% i.e. you were given additional 86% on Loan as Leverage so you will have to pay interest on ₹860000 (86%) of ₹5000×200 = ₹1000000 so as you hold the Futures

contract for 2 months you will have to pay 3+3=6% of ₹860000 = ₹51600 interest from your Capital gains.

As you gained ₹400000, you will have to deduct ₹51600 interest from it which will be ₹400000-₹51600 = ₹348400

Now, you invested ₹140000 but got in return ₹348400 which means a net profit of ₹348400-₹140000 = **₹208400** (excluding Tax)

As you saw, the Money just got 1.5× in just 2 months post payment of interest. This is the reason why it is so lucrative among Stock Market Traders. But, it also comes with an extremely High Risk which we will uncover in our next Scenario.

## **SCENARIO – II:**

Similar to Scenario – I, Let's suppose the Share Price falls down from ₹5000 to ₹3000/Share.

Then, it will be –

(₹3000-₹5000) × 200 = -₹400000

That means, you are now on a Loss of ₹400000+₹51600 (Interest) = ₹451600

Your Investment was ₹140000 and now you need to repay ₹451600, which means you need to pay an extra amount of ₹451600-₹140000=**₹311000** to your Stock Broker!!

The Harsh Reality is that just because of the Leverage being so Lucrative, People end up with no savings and more worse of having high Debt to be repaid to the Lenders may be apart from the Broker.

- **OPTIONS** – It is also a Derivative in the form of Contract which gives you the Right for a period of Time to exercise the Transaction at a particular Price.
  The Transaction which can be exercised is of two Types –

1. **CALL EUROPEAN (CE)** –

   It provides a Right to the Traders to 'Buy' an Underlying Asset such as Stocks, Commodity or Index at a particular Price for a defined Time Horizon.
   Whenever you 'Buy' a Call Option, you will need to give a 'Premium' to execute the Contract. Premium is nothing but the Token Amount which needs to be given to book the Option Contract. Remember that you always have an option to not 'Buy' if the Future Price prediction doesn't goes in your Favor, in that case the 'Premium' given will be the Loss.

Example –

Suppose Company A has a Share Price of ₹500 and a Person Buys a CE of 1 Lot (100 Shares) at a Premium of ₹10.

Now there could be 3 Possibilities, which is represented in the form of Tabular Chart bellow –

| Share Price | ₹500 | ₹510 | ₹550 |
|---|---|---|---|
| Profit/ Loss | -₹10 | ₹0 | ₹40 |

Here, in the First case we can see that the Price remains the same at the Expiry.
Thus, we cancel the order and only the 'Premium' deposited which here is ₹10 and it is the only Loss.
In second, the Price increases but just by ₹10 which is the Premium we paid to Book the order thus, we have no Loss/Profit.
Whereas. In Third case we see that Price moves up to +₹50 and -₹10 (Premium) gives us a Profit of ₹40.
Now, as it happens in the form of Lot sizes which in this case was 100 Shares means that, In First Case you have a Loss of ₹10×100 = ₹1000 and in Third Case, you have a Profit of ₹40×100 = ₹4000.

Now that means you put ₹10 (Premium) in 1 Lot (100 Shares) which is ₹1000 and gained ₹4000 which is 4x Money.

2. **PUT EUROPEAN (PE)** –
It is just reverse of Call European; here it provides the 'Right' to the traders to 'Sell' an Underlying Asset at a particular Price for a defined period of Time.
It is done when the option Buyer expect a downfall in Share Price.
Example –
Suppose Company A has a Share Price of ₹500 and a Person Buys a PE of 1 Lot (100 Shares) at a Premium of ₹10.

Now there could be 3 Possibilities, which is represented in the form of Tabular Chart bellow –

| Share Price | ₹500 | ₹490 | ₹450 |
|---|---|---|---|
| Profit/ Loss | -₹10 | ₹0 | ₹40 |

Similar to the previous Example of Call Option, you gain Profit/Loss. But as it seems to be very impressive because of Limited Risk and High Rewards but it is immensely addictive in nature and can convert into **Gambling** if not taken consideration of your emotions!!

Because you may think that what is the Loss in this case, ₹1000 Right? Wrong! You will book 10 Trades in order to make Profit and will end up losing ₹1000×10 = ₹10000 in a Trading Day and if you got addicted to it, can cost ₹10000/Trading Day ~ ₹250000/Month!!

You can execute transaction in Three Price Bands as –

IN THE MONEY (ITM) –
As the name suggests, it is an Order made on the Price which is already at its Intrinsic Value (Undervalued) and is already in Profit when ordered.

AT THE MONEY (ATM) –
When the Order is placed on the exact price of Stocks/Index/Commodity then, it is known as At the Money Order. The Profits can only be made when the Price increases more than (Present value +Premium).

OUT OF THE MONEY (OTM) –
When the Price is Over-valued and needs to move in the favorable Trend, in order to book Profits or else it is already in Loss when ordered.

Let us again try to understand in the form of Tabular Chart –

Suppose that the Share Price of Stock-A is ₹500 then, these could be the possible values of Options.

| Order/Type | ITM | ATM | OTM |
|---|---|---|---|
| CE | 480 | 500 | 520 |
| PE | 540 | 500 | 470 |

Option Premium is derived by two Components which are Intrinsic Value (Amount of the Option is ITM) and Time Value, which is calculated as –
(Premium – Intrinsic Value)

So, if the Option is ATM/OTM then, the Time Value will be equal to Premium as the Price is not 'Intrinsic Value' and thus it will be taken as 0.

Let us understand the Cost & Income in the 'Call/Put Option Buying and Selling'

<u>Strike Price</u> – Price at which Option is booked.
<u>Expiry Market Price</u> – When the Option Price expires.

So, For a Call Option Buyer:–

COST – Premium

INCOME – (Expiry Market Price - Strike Price - Premium)

For a Call Option Seller it is just the Reverse,
COST – (Expiry Market Price - Strike Price - Premium)

INCOME – Premium

In case of Put Option Buyer it will be,
COST – Premium

INCOME – (Strike Price – Expiry Market Price - Premium)

In case of Put Option Seller it will be,
COST – (Strike Price – Current Market Price - Premium)

INCOME – Premium

- **SWAPS –**
  Unlike of it being traded in Stock Market, it is a physical agreement between two parties to get mutually benefited by exchanging the Cash Flows or Liabilities from two different Financial Instruments.

These are of Four Types –

### INTEREST RATE SWAPS –
When two parties agree on exchanging the Interest Payment method, which usually involves Fixed Interest Rates for Floating Interest Rates to get mutually benefited through an agreement is known as Interest Rate Swap.

### CURRENCY SWAPS –
It is usually done in exchange of Foreign Currencies in order to hedge (protect) the deal from frequent Currency Fluctuations.

### COMMODITY SWAPS –
It is not the exchange of an actual Commodity, but is designed to exchange the Floating Cash Flows based on the Price of a Commodity against Fixed Cash Flow determined by the pre-agreed price of the Commodity.

### CREDIT DEFAULT SWAP –
The most Risky amongst all of them, it provides Insurance from the Default of a Debt Instrument. In this case, the Buyer transfers Premium payments to the Seller, whereas if the Asset defaults then, it will be transferred to Swap Seller.

Finally Completed, Yes, this was the most Tiring part of the entire Book to write.

I hope it was not difficult to understand as I tried my level to write in the most simplified way possible.

Perhaps, Basics of Trading got more detailed than expected. But, as it is said, Knowledge is never enough!

Now, let's jump right into the Investing in Stock Market. But before knowing the Techniques of Investment, we need to know basic structure of Stock Market, in India there are two Stock Exchange –

National Stock Exchange (NSE) & Bombay Stock Exchange (BSE) and here, Stocks of the Companies are listed for trading where, Exchange acts as a Marketplace of executing the Orders on behalf of the Sellers and Buyers.

Whenever you Buy/Sell the Shares of the Stocks then, you will see some terms as,

<u>REGULAR ORDER</u> – When you normally Buy/Sell Shares in the Stock Market.

<u>GTT (Good Till Triggered) ORDER</u> – When you 'Buy or Sell' Shares on a presumed Price, which when gets triggered

executes the order within 365 days of Timeline is known as GTT.

<u>MARKET OREDR</u> – When the Order to Buy or Sell the Shares is executed on the Current Market Price of the Share is known as Market Order.

<u>LIMIT ORDER</u> – When the Order is given on a pre-determined Price and only gets executed when the Price is triggered within the Trading Session (Mon-Fri 9:15AM-3:30PM).

<u>STOP LOSS</u> – As the name suggests, it is a setting through which you can stop your loss after a certain point which is set by you.

Now when you are aware of all the Important Terms, let's understand the techniques used to Invest in Stocks.
So, while purchasing a Stock we need to Analyze it and there are two ways of doing it, which are as Follows –

- **<u>FUNDAMENTAL ANALYSIS</u> –**
  This is done to identify the Stocks which are Sustainable and Profitable at its Business with future Growth prospects.

To do the Fundamental Analysis we will need to visit an Online Screener which helps us in Identification of those Stocks.
In a Stock Screener, put the Filters as –

<u>MARKET CAP</u> – It's the Market Capital of the Stock listed on Exchange, which in simple Terms means the present valuation of the Company. It is calculated as,
Market Cap = Current Stock Price × Total Outstanding Shares.
We should always be Alert of Micro sized Companies and consider Stocks with a Market Cap at least more than ₹1000 Crores.

<u>PE RATIO</u> – Price to Earnings (PE) Ratio is calculated as,
PE = (Current Market Price/Earnings per Share)
It signifies the amount of Money an Investor is willing to invest in a single share of a Company for ₹1 of its Earnings.
Thus, lower is the better but should not be very low. Ideally, a PE range of 1 to 20 is good.

<u>5Y HIST. REV. GROWTH</u> – 5 Years Historical Revenue Growth, as the name is self-sufficient and for a Business, steady

growth should be observed in terms of Revenue so that it could expand itself to a more large scale multi-dimensional or a Monopoly Business player of the Market.
Generally, more than 10% is considered a good and stable revenue growth.

<u>ROCE</u> – Return on Capital Employed is the Net Profit made on the Capital used in the Company. It is calculated in the form of,
ROCE = EBIT (Earnings before Interest and Tax) ÷ Capital Employed
It is seen that more than 15% is a decent value.

<u>FREE CASH FLOW</u> – It is the Money saved by the Companies after deducting the Investments made from Net Operating Profit after Taxes.
Considering Market Cap more than ₹1000 Crores having a Free Cash Flow of more than ₹10 Crore is a good sign.

<u>DEBT TO EQUITY</u> – It is a ratio which simply shows us the amount of Debt, Company has used to Finance its Asset.
It is calculated as,
Debt to Equity = Total Debt ÷ Total Asset

**PROMOTER HOLDING** – Simply the percentage of Shares, which the Owner of the Company owns.

No one knows the Business more than the Owner itself and thus, the more the holdings of the Owner, the more is the confidence of the Owner on its own Company.

If the Promoter Holdings are more than 60% is a great sign.

**ALPHA** – It is considered as an excess Return produced by the Stock according to its Benchmark, when adjusted for Risk.

Any value above 1 is considered good.

**BETA** – It is considered as the measure of Volatility in respect to the Market. Where, 1 means Stock moving parallel with the Market, More/Less than 1 means more/less volatile than Market.

It is preferred in the range of 0.50-1.50

**5Y EBITDA GROWTH** –
It is basically the Compounded Annual Growth (CAGR) of a Company's EBITDA over the past 5 years.

More than 10% is a decent growth.

**CLOSE PRICE** – Current Market Price

Apart from these Parameters, you should also check the Balance Sheet, Annual Reports and Market Analysis of the Sector to which the Stock belongs.

- **TECHNICAL ANALYSIS –**
  This is done to analyze the Stock if it is at its Intrinsic Value or it is overvalued. To analyze it, we need to understand Candlestick Patterns and Indicators which helps us in identification of the Trend Patterns. Accordingly, it helps us to take actions for Buying, Selling or Holding the Stocks.

  CANDLESTICK – It is a Candle Shaped indicator used to read the Price Trend according to the Transactions made in those particular stocks.
  In simple terms, when Stock Price moves in Upward direction due to Buying of Shares in a particular Price creates a 'Green Candle Stick' in that time frame and similarly, a 'Red Candle Stick' is formed when the Shares are Sold in a particular quantity in that Time Frame.
  It also creates certain patterns which are used for Trading and not much of a use in Investing.

RSI INDICATOR – Relative Strength Index is a Momentum Indicator used to measure the range of Price fluctuations as per being either Overbought or Oversold Zone.

By default, it has an Upper Limit of 70 and Lower Limit of 30, which can be changed in settings as 60 and 40 for Upper and Lower limit respectively.

After Applying this Indicator, you will see a range band bellow the Trading Chart which shows if the graph goes beyond the upper band means it is in 'Overbought Zone' whereas, if it crosses the lower band means it is in 'Oversold Zone'.

SUPERTREND INDICATOR –
As the name suggests, it is a Trend based Indicator which works on Average True Range (ATR) and its single line is created combining the Trend detection and Volatility in the Price of the Stock/Index being analyzed.

By default it has a setting of Length = 10 and Factor = 3 where, if we change the settings to Length = 14 will give more predictable Price Action movement.

It is simply analyzed by the lines formed following the Candlestick patterns where, Green Line means an indication of Uptrend whereas, Red Line means Downtrend.

## PIVOT POINTS –

This is the simplest Indicator to determine the Support (Position from which the Candlestick patterns may form an Uptrend) and Resistance (Position from which the Candlestick patterns may for a Downtrend) of the Share Price according to the Price Action Movement. It forms a line with symbols as $S1, S2....S_n$ which is the Support level and $R1, R2....R_n$ which is the Resistance level

Apart from these Indicators, there are plenty of more advanced Indicators used in Trading Setups. But, our Intention to learn Technical Analysis was to be able to determine the Trend of the Market to grab better Investing opportunities in a Share.

I hope you were able to understand the Concepts easily and will become a Great Investor, Always remember that never invest all your Money into a Single Asset but try diversifying it as per your Risk Appetite.

I would suggest not investing more than 30% of Total Investments in Stocks as it being Highly Unpredictable!

# IF YOU HAVE ANY SUGGESTIONS REGARDING A NEW TOPIC/SUBJECT PLEASE SEND ME, I SHALL DEFINITELY LOOK AFTER IT......

Contact for suggestions on my email – singhsrijan890@gmail.com

This Book comes with a Hidden Cash back of ₹50 which can be availed by sending ₹1 on My UPI Id – (Iamsrijansingh@upi) and get ₹51 back to your Account.
Also don't forget to send the Pic of the Book on my Gmail given above!

## REFERENCES:

[1] BYJUS – (Ch-1, Pg – 10-13 *Types of Banks*)

[2] RBI – (Ch-1, Pg – 16 *DIGC ACT*)

[3] SBI INTERNET BANKING – (Ch-2, Pg-22 *Interest rates*)

[4] INDIA POST BANKS – (Ch-2, Pg-30, 39 *Interest rates*)

[5] SBI WEALTH – (Ch-3, Pg - 49-50, 62, 69, 103 *Formula to calculate R.D, S.I.P, F.V, E.M.I*)

[6] HDFC LIFE – (Ch-5, Pg – 94-95 *Types of Health Insurance*)

[7] POLICY BAZAAR – (Ch-5, Pg-96 *Types of Vehicle Insurance*)

[8] CLEARTAX – (Ch-6, Pg – 104 *Taxation Rules*)

[9] NATIONAL STOCK EXCHANGE – (Ch-7, Pg – 110 *Market Size of Index as of June 2024*)

[10] NIFTYINDICES – (Ch-6, Pg – 111-115 *Performance of 15yrs of Nifty Indices from January 2009-2024*)

[11] ETMONEY – (Ch-6, Pg – 122-130 Performance of 11yrs of DSP Energy, SBI Healthcare, ICICI Technology Fund from 2013-2024)

[12] ICRA – (Ch-6, Pg – 130-131 Types of Credit Rating provided by a Credit Risk Agency)

[13] MONEYCONTROL – (Ch-6, Pg – 137-143 ROI generated in Different Funds over specified period of time)

[14] ETMONEY – (Ch-6, Pg – 146-147 Details about ICICI Prudential Retrement Fund, Pg – 148 HDFC Children's Gift Fund)

[15] GROWW – (Ch-6, Pg – 156-157 Details about Nippon India ETF Nifty 50 BeES, ICICI Prudential US Bluechip Equity Direct Fund, SBI Gold Fund )

[16] CORPORATEFINANCEINSTITUTE – (Ch-7, Pg – 163-164, 168, 171, 173-174 About Derivatives and its Classifications)

[17] INVESTOPEDIA – (Ch – 7, Pg – 178-179, 181-182 Ratios and Indicators)

www.ingramcontent.com/pod-product-compliance
Lightning Source LLC
Chambersburg PA
CBHW052254220526
45471CB00001B/327